MORGAN'S YORKSHIRE

Morgan's Yorkshire

John Morgan

Illustrated by Cluff

First published in 2000 *by*
Smith Settle Ltd
Ilkley Road
Otley
West Yorkshire
LS21 3JP

© Yorkshire Post Newspapers Ltd & John Morgan 2000
Illustrations © Cluff 2000

ISBN 1 85825 140 0

British Library Cataloguing-in-Publication Data:
A catalogue record for this book is available from
the British Library

Set in Monotype Sabon

Designed, printed and bound by
SMITH SETTLE
Ilkley Road, Otley, West Yorkshire LS21 3JP

Contents

Foreword

John Morgan has drawn on a vast store of anecdotes and personal memories to create this wonderfully entertaining book. For half a century and more he was a member of the editorial team at the *Yorkshire Evening Post,* and colleagues regarded him with wonder, so many were his various manifestations. His roles included that of the racing editor, Ranger, whose successful tips were signalled by the insertion of a standing slug of lead type in race-meeting results, 'Winner was Ranger's selection'. He was a determined reporter, at ease whether talking to characters such as Woodbine Lizzie, or successive Lord Mayors of Leeds.

His 'Sporting Yorkshire' column was a prodigy of wit, gossip and information, and produced in such volume that one of the *Post*'s printers suggested papering the case-room with his galley proofs. He also ventured into theatre criticism. On top of all this, John was regularly called on to speak at sporting dinners and charitable events, where he frequently convulsed his audiences with his stories and reminiscences.

For many readers of the *Evening Post*, his easy writing style provided welcome relaxation after a busy day, and he was like a friendly neighbour who dropped in most nights with something interesting to say. This book is drawn from a Monday column featured in the *Post* in the latter part of his career, in which he tapped a prodigious gusher, his memories of a busy lifetime. The compilation will delight old friends and create many new ones.

Newspapermen who knew him will also turn to it with interest. We are beyond being surprised by Johnny Morgan's achievements and versatility, and by turning his hand to a book, he has made a logical progression from the more transient medium of newsprint. Awestruck, we now await the film.

Malcolm Barker
Editor of the Yorkshire Evening Post, *1970-1987*

Preface

It was hammered into me in the early stages of my journalistic career that there is nothing as dead as yesterday's news — 'not even the Dodo!'. But it is possible to argue with the death sentence imposed on stories twenty-four hours old.

Thoughts still dwell on characters, celebrated and otherwise, who added indelible incidents to newspaper columns decades ago. Memories of their respective contributions remain fresh and captivating today.

Nostalgia is not a thing of the past, as I regularly proved in my *Yorkshire Evening Post* feature called 'Morgan's Yorkshire' devoted to the 'bad-old-good-old days'. Recollections of nights at the 'flicks', tripping the light fantastic at local ballrooms, the home-spun humour of music hall comics, rationing, the blackout and old-fashioned remedies for all manner of maladies drew the desired response from thousands of appreciative readers.

Nearly six decades as a newspaper hack, concentrating on the sporting scene, was an acceptable challenge but lacked fun. Sport unfortunately remains a serious subject. There is no levity in losing. It was not until I delved into the world of Zambuk, Doctor Blaud's Pink Pills for Pale People, Woodbine Lizzie, Granelli's ice-cream, Leeds City Varieties, Albert Modley, Ronnie Hilton and old-fashioned policing that we struck a rich vein of humour. It gave me unqualified job satisfaction — a feeling even more rewarding than a handsome increase in salary.

'It made me laugh and cry at the same time' was the reaction of one reader. I have selected a series of such stories at random for inclusion in this book, and if they raise a smile or touch the tear ducts, this author will be a happy man. Here is simply a meander down that hackneyed but fitting description 'Memory Lane'. There's more to come, dear reader. Yesterday's news has not been cremated.

Dedicated to my wife Maureen

Return to Cleethorpes

Cleethorpes beckoned me recently for the first time in sixty-odd — perhaps very odd — years when I was asked to speak at a local sporting club's delightful dinner, and it reminded me of an episode in my early childhood.

Over half-a-century ago, Cleethorpes was the place my Auntie Maud Appleyard always took her bairns for a day trip and, although I pride myself on an elephantine memory, I admit that I have only vague recollections of my inclusion in one of her regular seaside sorties. Auntie Maud worked for the late Joe Huddlestone, whose rhubarb fields spread for countless acres round the Castleford-Methley area. When she was not picking that palatable produce, she was engaged in 'pea pulling', and that job description will revive a back-aching era for those old enough to remember the arduous occupation.

I once walked past a rhubarb field and swear I heard the leafy stalks muttering: 'People, people, people ...' And I have always had an appetite for 'tuskey', which gave rise to one of the oldest music hall jokes. How often did you hear the red-nosed comic ask his straight man: 'What do you put on your rhubarb?' The stooge replied: 'Manure'. And the comedian would bring the house down with the tag-line: 'We put custard on ours'.

Auntie Maud was a kindly soul and a chapel-goer who knelt at her bedside to say her night prayers. She had the gift of making children feel special and personally welcome, and was possessive to a point of greeting me with a hug and the delighted cry: 'It's our John!' It made me feel wanted. I was not 'yours' but 'ours'. She always wore a floral pinafore, and when she pulled your shining little face on to her 'pinny', you enjoyed being suffocated with love and a feeling of complete and utter security.

But the theme is Cleethorpes, where I went with Auntie Maud in the early 1930s, and I was often told afterwards that I disgraced myself. This was before the days of disposable nappies or diapers, as I heard one lady describe them the other day. It was long before the advent of paddy-pants and plastic knickers. Little lads had bottoms covered with any material that would hold water. Babies looked like Sabu the Elephant Boy or a mini Tarzan of the Apes as they ran around in their primitive and well-pinned loin cloths.

But I was dressed to kill the day I went to Cleethorpes. I was like Little Lord Fauntleroy, with sun-bonnet over a mass of fair curls, blue velvet top with trim lace collar, matching pants — over the nappy — ankle socks, sandals, and clutching the inevitable bucket and spade.

I disgraced myself. I lost the offensive, well-filled, matching pants — and nappy — as I attempted to fill my pail from the edge of the rippling waters. They headed out for the ocean on the River Humber to form one of the first oil slicks or start the pollution we now read so much about. And I finished building my sandcastles with Auntie Maud's headsquare wrapped round my otherwise naked nether regions.

The story was told in our family circle for decades!

Mick the Mongrel and Trudy the Poodle

Mick — our mutt of a mongrel — was never pampered, powdered or permed like many of the cosseted canine candidates in the Crufts competition, which made its initial bow (wow) over a hundred years ago. But if Mick had lived to be twice that age, he would never have been accepted for the contest to determine the country's top dog.

Mick was a happy little ruffian who held his own in a locality in which any dog without a tattered ear, half-chewed tail or similar battle scar was classed as a tourist. Mick was loved. He was walked and watered, and he wagged what was left of his docked rudder in appreciation of our regular bouts of tummy-tickling. You could almost hear him giggling.

Mick also had his moments of joy with the opposite gender. And I recall a rather upper-crust neighbour shedding tears of anguish as she bitterly condemned Mick's persistent wooing of her darling Trudy.

Trudy was a prima donna of a Parisienne poodle. She had no right to flaunt her appealing aristocracy in front of the Heinz varieties of doggies whose only claim to fame was that they were on personal terms with every tree and lamp post on the Gipton Estate. Trudy's genteel owner wept bitterly over Mick's courting of her Trudy, who had a pedigree as long as Wykebeck Valley Road. The owner dabbed her eyes and wailed:

'She's ruined. She's scarred forever. My Princess of Purity will never be the same.'

And I swear that there was a self-satisfied smirk on Mick's soft brown face and his eyes sparkled as we listened to the scandalised lady's condemnation of his philandering.

Trudy was all pom-poms and pink ribbons. Mick was a plain, multi-blooded tramp of a terrier. He had simple tastes. He had a passion for ratting on the banks of Monkey Beck, burying bones, and joining in cricket and football games, when he was not cavorting with ladies.

Mick — son of a Leeds market bitch called Floss — fostered his liaison with Trudy in a romp near our sunken Anderson air-raid shelter. We waited with increasing anticipation for Trudy to produce her litter. But we never saw them.

The rather snobbish lady — from her Ena Sharples hairnet down to her open-toed sandals — flitted with the pet who failed to show dogged resistance to Mick's overtures.

Mick was the type who would eat owt. He was not finicky about his food. He was so unlike a dog of my acquaintance who responded to the name William Calvert and relished beans on toast. William Calvert ate nothing else, and he preferred Bachelors Beans to others, and liked his toast brown and buttered as opposed to burnt and dry. William Calvert was a one-off character. And so was Mick, who was just one in a long line of assorted quadrupeds to be welcomed into the Morgan household.

I am sure that strays had our address. They simply turned up on the doorstep and, within seconds of being admitted, they had booked full board and lodgings for the rest of their natural. Many brought nothing with them but their own fleas, and one crazy mixed-up dog of doubtful parentage had to be fumigated before he was allowed to join a family he quickly learned to dominate.

I come from a long line of animal lovers. We would not exactly go ga-ga over gorillas or crazy over crocodiles. But dogs, cats, rabbits, hens, guinea pigs, not forgetting spiders, caterpillars, budgies, etcetera, have all sampled our largesse and become a responsibility and occasionally a liability.

For instance, what do you do with a caterpillar called Clarence when you go on holiday? Do you take him with you in his matchbox stuffed with cabbage leaves, or do you order the kids to bid him a tearful goodbye and force them to release him into the back garden? We reluctantly opted for choice number two, and that is the last we saw of our Clarence.

But dogs are a different kettle of fish, if you follow and pardon the analogy. I remember the story of a love-sick young swain who walked hand-in-hand through the fields near his home. The youth's dog trotted along in front, and suddenly a bitch came into view. The pair greeted each other with affectionate nuzzling of noses. And the lad turned to the object of his desire and sighed.

'That makes me want to do the same.'

The girl returned his gaze and murmured:

'Well why don't you? After all, it is your dog, isn't it?'

But gentlemen do not always have more love and respect for ladies than dogs. In Sheffield in 1806 a chap parted with his wife for two guineas and a dog. We are told that all parties were satisfied with the outcome of the negotiations and that the dog did not object to his sudden change of ownership.

It is rather more difficult to sell a surplus wife these days, and one can also experience problems when it comes to passing on unwanted puppies — especially if the mum produces more than an average crop of extra mouths to feed. But a pal of mine hit on a sure-fire system after the birth of eleven pups. Six weeks later he advertised in the local newspaper: 'Free to good home — eleven adorable puppies.'

There was no response. Not even a single inquiry. So he changed the wording: 'Free to good home — one very ugly and ten extremely pretty puppies.'

Within hours of publication, his telephone never stopped ringing. All the callers wanted the 'ugly' one and, by the end of the following day, he had given away the 'ugly' pup eleven times.

I have never been to Crufts. It isn't my scene. It wasn't our Mick's either. He always ran a mile at the mere mention of grooming. And he disappeared for hours on end at the sight of a bath and soapy water. But the smelly hound was still the country's top dog to me — and to many others who fell for the appealing charm of this mutt of a mongrel.

Bless Them All

Do you know what happened on the 15th September 1940? The sky above our green and pleasant land was clear of German aeroplanes for the first time in weeks. And the celebrated Few — to whom Winston Churchill told us so many of us owed so much — had won the Battle of Britain. We will always salute the glorious memory of such a fighting force. And we will recall with pride, and eternal gratitude, the courageous stand the flower of our youth made for mankind.

I was a child and did not entirely comprehend what was happening to the world. But we realised that life was different, with talk of evacuating kiddies to safer places, the provision of gas masks in cardboard boxes, and the issue of ration cards and clothing coupons. We faced years of austerity. But the traditional stiff upper lip, and inherent sense of humour, kept us ticking over and making the best of a heartbreaking chapter in the history of this blessed island.

There was even mirth in evacuation. I recall a group of my friends saying a tearful goodbye to mums as they boarded buses in Leeds to take them to the safety of far-away Tadcaster. It must have been all of fourteen miles away from home. But it seemed like the other side of the world to mothers and offspring, who embraced as though they would never again have the opportunity to clasp each other. Before I could join in the adventure, my mates returned. The powers that be decided Leeds was a much safer place than Tadcaster and families were happily reunited.

Of course, we had the Home Guard to protect us. When it was first launched, it had the initials LDV for Local Defence Volunteers. And one irreverent soul called them the Look, Duck and Vanish brigade. They were kitted out with broom handles and they sported armbands as they waited for First World War rifles, ill-fitting khaki tunics and baggy pants to arrive. Weekends usually provided the most convenient hours for Dad's Army to embark on manoeuvres. It became the norm to step out of the front door and watch half a dozen elderly men — with boot-polished faces and clutching their broom handles — leopard-crawling round privet hedges.

The air-raids spawned many a good yarn, and one tale was often told of the lady who jumped from her bed when the siren sounded. She could not switch on the light for fear of piercing the black-out and her fingers scratched across the bedside table in a frantic search.

'What are you looking for?' inquired her husband.

'My false teeth', she replied.

'Nay', he said, 'never mind your teeth. They're dropping bombs, not pork pies.'

I can't vouch for the authenticity of the incident. But I recall that my Aunt Eliza never went to the shelter without dressing to the nines. She put on her best coat, feather boa, Ascot-type hat, and gripped her favourite leather handbag, containing rosary beads, insurance policies and so on, and walked as stately as royalty to the haven. When asked why she always put on her finery, Aunt Eliza answered:

'If I am going to meet my maker, I want to be dressed for the occasion.'

One night we refused to go to our back-garden shelter, and we grouped under the front room table, with the same aunt leading prayers for our safety, when we suddenly heard explosions and the sound of breaking glass.

'We are being machine gunned', hollered one of the kids.

And we screamed with fear. But a brave sortie to the pantry, from where the noises emanated, revealed that vibrations from the local ack-ack firing had caused three dozen bottles of rhubarb wine to explode. The corks flew in all directions and the contents flooded the kitchen.

The morning after a nocturnal visit by the Luftwaffe always signalled a search for shrapnel, and we had an elderly neighbour, Mr Foley, who repaired broken slates and often found bits and pieces of shells stuck on the rooftops. He gave them to us for souvenirs.

The pensioner lived with his daughter, and he was involved in one incident his family will never forget. The sirens blasted their banshee wail. And he was forced from his bed. He tucked his shirt lap into his trousers and in his drowsy state also pushed the bottom of the bedroom curtains down his pants. When he started to walk, the drapes pulled down the curtain pole, which struck him at the back of his head.

He fell down (pole-axed) and shouted to his daughter: 'Get the kids out, Agnes, I'm hit.'

We laughed for days over that. It did us good to have a giggle. Hitler failed to halt our cheerful acceptance of the ever-increasing adversities.

Do you remember the black flour, and how our mothers used to riddle it with sieves or muslin cloths to take out the rough bits and produce a white, softer-textured flour? Those husks and indigestible bits of rough stuff are now called fibre and highly recommended by health experts. But we were not aware of the benefits. We preferred home-baked white bread and dreamed of the day when we would be able to buy real eggs instead of the dried variety, and when children would see a banana for the first time and enjoy the other fruits of the life we now take for granted

Our men won the Battle of Britain, and we had another five years of war and bloodshed. We did owe the 'Magnificent Few' the debt Winston Churchill outlined and we will never forget those who came after to make the supreme sacrifice. They ensured that this country would not surrender to the Nazi jackboot. And they made it possible that we would be able to recall, with tears, the ways of the war and the days when laughter was our safety valve. God bless them all.

White Roses and Cane Snaps

Do you celebrate Yorkshire Day with justifiable pride in your birthright? Do you sport the white rose, devour double helpings of our world-acclaimed pudding, and lapse into dialect peculiar to the Broad Acres?

I proclaim to all in earshot my fierce allegiance to all things Yorkshire but — God forgive me — I can't do it in the vernacular. I draw the line when it comes to 'ee bah gum' and phrases like: 'Appen tha cooms from 'Uddersfeld, doosta?' I am a sloppy speaker and fracture the Queen's English with the best. But I confess to horror-stricken readers the scandalous admission that I prefer 'don't you?' to 'doosta?'

I left my native Castleford, as a curly-haired five year old, for a home in Leeds, and I was quite an attraction at my new school. Children gathered at playtime to hear me swear and speak with honest, rounded, Yorkshire vowels. 'Me booits' and 'Ah sed nowt o' t' sort' — plus a few sentences like 'get theesen ower 'ere' — were listened to by an admiring audience. And my venial sinning swearwords drew gasps of wonderment from greatly impressed listeners.

The colourful turn of phrase was the norm at my first infant school — Hightown, Castleford — where the story is still told of a young teacher who vowed she would improve the diction, vocabulary and the general elocution standard of her diminutive pupils.

She signalled to little Billy to stand and give her a sentence pertaining to the previous evening. Billy came from a large family. His school uniform was a case of 'first up — best dressed'. He wore the accepted jersey buttoned at the neck, covering shirt and braces, with short trousers rubbing his knees, and stockings wrinkled over the tops of well-scuffed boots. Billy drew himself to his full height of three feet nothing and intoned:

'Last neet I went t' fish oil.'

He beamed his satisfaction and resumed his seat. Miss bristled. She slapped the top of her desk with a ruler and hollered:

'It is not "neet", it is "night". And it is not "fish oil". What is it, children?'

The class rose as one and chanted in unison:

'It's fish hole, miss.'

Billy was the same pupil, picked at random by the mental arithmetic teacher who asked:

'Your mother has half a dozen eggs in the pantry and six rashers of bacon. How many is that altogether?'

Billy answered truthfully:

'When I came to school this morning, we'd neither bacon or eggs in the pantry cupboard, or anywhere else.'

I never had a 'Miss' to teach me. It was left to good nuns to correct my tendency to employ 't' hart', 'dooan't t' owd' and so on. And they also abolished with the threat of fire and brimstone my lapses into language a mite stronger.

They were kindly sisters, although one or two scorned the cane and slipper for an infinitely more painful administration of discipline. If you haven't had the lobe of your ear tugged by a nun as your scampering feet followed her swirling skirts to the front of the class, you have not sampled real agony. The pinched member reddens, burns and tingles for hours, and it is an experience only a masochist would be eager to repeat.

Being a little toadie, I rarely sampled the 'ear-ache', but recall with crystal clarity a day when Sister gave me an extra 'ear-wigging'. I was a milk monitor, and it was my job — on a cold morning — to bring the half-pint bottles and stack them round the coke-burning fire.

'This will take the chill from it', smiled our benign tutor.

We little thought in those days what bacteria we were arousing in our mid-morning beverage by bringing it to a tepid warmth. However, on that fateful morning I dropped a bottle and it smashed to smithereens. It is impossible to imagine how much floor space a modest half-pint of milk can cover. It was like a flood.

Sister let out a squeal of anger. She grabbed my ear in a pincer-like grip and pulled me up the corridor to the head-teacher's study. By the time we arrived I was climbing up the wall and the nun's wimple.

The cane was also a deterrent, but not for those who discovered a stone with magical properties. It was a glassy, smooth rock known as 'cane-snap', and we believed that if you rubbed it on your palms the cane would break on impact. I was nominated our school's first guinea pig. My canings averaged one a day, and always for the same offence — talking, with or without a Yorkshire accent.

The 'cane-snap' was applied. I did my level best to invite the stick, but Sir appeared to be oblivious to my non-stop conversation with anyone prepared to listen. Perhaps Sir had heard of 'cane-snap' and the embarrassing consequence for those who apply punishment.

Eventually Sir cottoned on. I was summoned for a whacking, but I winked with glee at those sharing deep confidence in 'cane-snap'. Two searing stripes across each hand quickly dispelled that conviction. I almost hit the ceiling and the weals were visible for a couple of hours. I am afraid the 'cane-snap' did not work for me or anyone else.

Our teachers had to exert authority, since we were not the best-behaved students. But perhaps they deprived us of a little of our Yorkshire heritage when they substituted 'Where are you going?' for 'Weer's t' bahn?'

Many is the time I 'talk Yorkshire' for fun. I gaze at the Lovely Maureen, extend my arms, and holler: 'Coom 'ere and givus a cuddle, treasure.' I call her treasure because of her sunken chest, and she will murder me — her toy boy — for that remark. But we enjoy Yorkshire Day as a Yorkshire couple should. We express gratitude that we were born in a unique county of breathtaking beauty.

Such a Moving Experience

It was a moving experience. Many described it as 'flitting'. Others termed it 'doing a moonlight'. It was a regular occurrence in the so-called good old days when rampant unemployment resulted in dire distress and wholesale rent arrears. Many families were forced to beat a hasty retreat to another place of sanctuary rather than face the demanding rent collector's threatening knock on the door and the inevitable disgrace of public eviction. Landlords were often identikit figures of ruthless Sir Jasper, the avaricious villain of many a tear-jerking melodrama.

In real life it was even more dramatic and heartbreaking, with skint tenants loading their pathetic possessions on to handcarts and stealing away in the middle of the night — hence the phrase 'doing a moonlight'.

Nowadays we crack gags about being poor. Comedians claim: 'We were so poor, my mother sold clothes pegs to gypsies. But we were well off compared to the family next door. Oxfam fed them. One of their kids was stamped "Made in Hong Kong", and his mother asked us if she could borrow our joint of beef to make some gravy.'

It is all a big giggle. But 'flitting' — enforced or otherwise — has never been a laughing matter. There is always sadness when you leave a home, even if you are improving your lot.

I recall the pangs of regret when the Lovely Maureen and our children quit the six shillings and fourpence a week rented one-up-and-one-down in Woodsley Place off Burley Road, Leeds, for the brand-new £1,750 semi-detached dwelling in Moor Flatts Road, Middleton. And I recall the tears when we later said goodbye to the real people of South Leeds to join the swells in North Leeds.

The 'moonlight' escapades were quite different, and if those fleeing from the landlord could afford something better than a hand-propelled cart, they hired Tom O'Brien's coal conveyance and his trusty horse Mick O'Brien. Mick was ready for the knacker's yard years before he actually departed to the horsey heaven known as the Elysian Fields. He was a good servant to Tom. He had huge blinkers. He was well-behaved. And his job was eased when Tom equipped his hitherto iron-rimmed cartwheels with pneumatic tyres. You could not hear the 'moonlighters' making their nocturnal escapes. But we did one night.

The neighbours and their six children made a human chain, and passed along bric-a-brac from the house to the cart. They heaved on a horsehair sofa — the one that prickled the back of the knees when you wore short trousers — and they stowed on a table, a couple of cane-bottomed chairs, a tasseled pelmet, pot dogs, flying geese and the aspidistra in a brass plant-pot holder.

All of a sudden there was an urgent whisper: 'Take care with the chandelier'. Would you believe it — a chandelier indeed. And so it appeared — a myriad of glass droplets with upturned holders of candle-shaped lightbulbs. The kids did not heed the muttered warning. There was a crash. The chandelier was in a million pieces, and the noise galvanised Mick O'Brien into galloping action. He gave a fair imitation of a Grand National runner as he pounded down Draper Street, the Bank, Leeds 9, and woke the neighbourhood to the fact that 'the chap and his wife with the six kids were doing a moonlight flit'.

Taste of Paradise for Joker Bert

Do you believe in the hereafter? I do, of course, but, unlike Bert who often holds court in the local snug, I have no idea what shape or form Paradise will take.

Bert reckons that he has already been through the Pearly Gates, and when he first launched into a description of Heaven — with all its celestial facilities — our initial reaction was to prise the pint of liquid sunshine from his limpet grip. But he is quite serious when he talks about having had a preview of his eternal reward. He sincerely believes that he has sampled the delights of his eventual destination.

It all stems back to the night he was persuaded to attend a theatre where a famous hypnotist topped the bill. Bert had no thoughts about joining the other volunteers on stage. He has never been a show-off. But it appears that he was one of the first to succumb to the 'influence'. And he walked slowly — with vacant expression and eyes staring — to the podium where he obeyed all manner of commands. Bert's wife assures him that he talked like a baby and wrote as he did when he was six years old. And she — and the rest of the audience — saw him leap from his chair every time the hypnotist suggested that his seat was on fire. But Bert has no recollection of such antics. All he can remember is taking a trip to Heaven, and he describes it as 'A bit like Butlins with angels, and all pink and fluffy'.

Bert is sure that it has a betting shop and, if it hasn't, he will be greatly disappointed, because no-one indulges in more tenpence doubles and trebles that this inveterate follower of the fluctuating fortunes of the country's equine thoroughbreds.

'I have been supporting sick horses for years', Bert laughs. 'The trouble is, I didn't know they were poorly until I backed them.'

But Bert doesn't chortle when he talks of 'going over the other side'. And he tends to get a trifle morbid when he recalls his first experience of 'passing over' and certain scenes from his childhood — not unknown to me.

I remember the wakes that used to be held on the Bank and the Gipton in Leeds when I was an impressionable — and often frightened — youngster. They were vigils kept on the deceased with, I presume, the object of 'waking' the person if the doctor had made a mistake and the prostrate victim had not really breathed his or her last.

Some of the wakes developed into hilarious and noisy shindigs. They didn't have bands or instrumentalists, but there was plenty of drink available and incredible stories galore. I remember playing hide the button and other games, and also recall one occasion when a man pulled on a headsquare and did a fair imitation of Old Mother Riley and his daughter Kitty. He took both parts and had the assembled mourners in stitches. I thought it was disrespectful and bordering on sacrilegious. But the adults obviously knew better than me.

Wakes were a custom — and an accepted part of living and dying. The mood always changed on the morning of the funeral. The immediate hours before the ceremony saw the laughter give way to tears and sobs. Men stood bare-headed as the cortège prepared to move from the house and head for church. Ladies folded black shawls round their head and shoulders, and the hymns — almost inaudible at first — grew into a wailing crescendo which sent shivers up the spine. The eerie sound lives with me today when I dwell on those scenes of death and distress.

However, Bert was in full flight again last weekend. At least he knows that a place has been reserved for him 'up there'. He predicts that one or two of us will finish 'down yonder', and it will serve us right for scoffing at his tales from the other side.

But we know he is leg puller. He has a wicked sense of humour, and he kept a straight face when he told us of four pals who made a pact to look after each other when the final call came. They deliberated on the question of whether cash would be required in the next world, and they decided that it would be as well to place a few pounds in the coffin of the first one to depart. Joe was put to his rest, and Jim solemnly placed £100 in notes at the side of his dear departed friend. Bill placed another £100 in 'readies' and Paddy — inspired — wrote a cheque for £300 and pocketed the other £200.

'It was a smart move by Paddy', Bert said. 'The others knew that they had been conned, but they would not admit the fact and they waited for developments.'

Sure enough, when Paddy got his next bank statement he discovered — to his utter amazement — that the cheque had been paid in and his account was £300 lighter.

'What he didn't know', added Bert 'was that the undertaker was a Yorkshireman, and a shrewd one at that.'

Do you believe in the hereafter? I do of course, but I'm not quite ready for the journey. I think I'll hang on for a few more years — and I advise you to do the same.

Nitty Nora, the Bug Explorer

It takes some believing, but it is absolutely true. And I felt a proper nana.

It happened in the barber's shop — or hairdressing salon as we now know them — and I still haven't recovered from the embarrassment. I had my locks washed and clipped. Suddenly the hairdresser produced a pink hairnet which he stretched on my head. I felt like Ena Sharples. In fact I looked like Ena Sharples. I closed my eyes, murmuring inwardly: 'I only hope no one sees me'. He then added injury to insult by levelling a perfumed spray at my blow-waved coiffure. The sickly aroma almost knocked me over. I doubt if I will patronise the glass and glitter emporium again. The barber did a nice job. But the net was a gross aggravation, and if you will pardon the pun, the scented finale was not to be sniffed at.

My thoughts went back to the days of my childhood when a couple of pennies paid for a swift, painless operation. There was no finesse, no happy chat, no flicking of comb and scissors. It was akin to shearing sheep: a quick zip, zip, and you emerged almost scalped by the barber's clippers.

My fellow was called Hoppy. He wasn't qualified. He didn't even have a shop. He ran his business from the scullery of his council house, and he was never short of well-shorn customers. But the cut-price crops came to an end when a claim was substantiated that, if you didn't have head lice when you arrived in his kitchen, you certainly had a few before you departed.

Every school had a Nitty Nora (the Bug Explorer) in those days. She was the nurse who paid regular visits to run her fingernails over your scalp. You lived in mortal dread of teacher calling you to the front of the class and handing you a 'nit note' to take home. The unfortunate lads who received the missives could always be picked out. They would turn up for lessons the following day with just a tiny tuft of hair stuck above the forehead and the rest of the head shaven.

I can honestly say — and I am not being smug — that I never had a note. But by golly I remember the smell of endless head washing with evil-smelling soap (wasn't it Derbac?) and the hours draped over my mother's apron as she scratched and scraped with a fine-toothed comb.

We used to have a visiting barber in Castleford. Outside baths were the norm in hot summers. Women filled the peggy tub with hot soapy water and a dash of dolly-blue. And it was often said that the kids went in first, followed by the whippets, and finally the grandad. After the ablutions, the children queued for the summer short back and sides and, occasionally, short front and top as well. We looked like a row of Kojaks.

There were other styles, like the pudding cut, which necessitated the placing of a batter-mixing bowl on the head of the 'victim'. The barber would then use his hand shears up to the rim. Those clippers were instruments of torture. They often jammed with a lump of hair and flesh between the blades. And some were so blunt, they didn't cut the hair, they dragged it out.

One of my favourite haunts was Barber Green's shop. You not only had a cheap haircut but you were acquainted with the latest news from the boxing front, because he was not only a hairdresser of great repute but a top referee. The walls of his premises were festooned with pictures of scrappers in various fighting poses, and he would talk for hours of the toughness, talents and resilience of Benny Lynch, Jackie Patterson, Jimmy Wilde and other famous pugilists, as he snipped away at your healthy growth. There was always a good supply of boxing magazines to wile away the waiting. And you would also relish the *Picture Post, John Bull* and other long-gone publications.

When your turn arrived, Barber Green motioned you to perch in the chair. It went up and down with his foot pressure. And he flicked a sheet round your neck with the sweeping expertise of a matador twirling his cape. He was another zip-zip-zip merchant, and he finished you off by scraping a razor down the nape of your neck and blowing talc from a rubber container which puffed the cooling powder on to your reddening skin. He would then apply brilliantine, which gave you the look of an out-of-work Italian tenor, or rub on a dollop of a thick, slimy, green concoction which plastered the hair to the head and set like concrete. It was no good saying you didn't want it. You got it. And you returned home looking for all the world like Lord Snooty, with your dad saying: 'Now that's what I call a haircut'.

It was only in your teens that you really started to adopt a hairstyle and dictate how you wanted it cutting and shaping. You often saw notices outside shops stating 'Army haircuts repaired', and there was a shortage of suitable hairdressing during my austerity-ridden youth.

The best tonsorial tale of all comes from former rugby league referee Billy Thompson, who is renowned for a fierce hairstyle. His high back and sides are almost shaved. He officiated in one game when one rough forward attempted to obliterate another. His unfortunate opponent was poleaxed, prostrate, out to the world. Billy walked across to remonstrate with the puncher, who said:

'I never touched him, ref.'

'There's only thee and me in striking distance', Billy replied, 'and I swear that I didn't do him.'

He pulled out his notebook, and the hard man suddenly collapsed in a fit of uncontrollable giggles.

'What are you laughing at?' asked Billy.

The chap almost burst with mirth. 'Who cut your ruddy hair, ref?' he guffawed.

And Billy forgot to book him.

Happy haircuts, and try and dodge the green stuff. It will cement bricks!

Famous Last Words

The least of my faithful and forgiving band of admirers was a chap who used to cut out my articles. He pasted them on a long length of wallpaper before scribbling in bold letters 'Famous Last Words' across stories I had literally dragged from my soul. My reluctant fan would then roll the strip into the thickness of a broomstick and post it to my office.

I never discovered his identity. But I did not extend any malice because he was fully entitled to his opinion of my pathetic attempts at journalism. And he expressed his view of the end product with a gesture he obviously considered to be appropriate to his sentiments. Because he never appended his name, he became known to our mailroom staff as FLW, and the chap in charge of the post used to holler: 'There's another from FLW for you, John. He's a card isn't he?'

Unfortunately, for those who liked a titter at my discomfiture — but fortunately for me — the mystery missives from Famous Last Words suddenly stopped. And he gradually disappeared from my thoughts and affection until the other day, when I came across a list of well-used expressions under the heading — you've guessed it — Famous Last Words. They usually precede accidents, and here is a sample:

'It was my right of way; There's a quicker way to do it; I can do this with my eyes shut; You don't have to switch the electricity off if you know what you are doing; No thanks I can lift it myself; It looks strong enough to hold my weight.'

The last two examples of FLW are based on strength, and this is the crux of my story. I went to school with a kid who was so tough he chewed nails and spat out rust. He had muscles on his muscles. He shaved when he was thirteen years old. He once reduced a full set of bar-room furniture to sawdust. And I envied him his physique — I was the original five stone weakling. I have always admired feats of great strength, and I have interviewed men who would have dwarfed Samson. Geoff Capes is one. And before I met a renowned Leeds giant, Barry Anderson, I thought that a nail was a small piece of pointed metal which was used to take aim before lowering a hammer on to the thumb. Barry bent six inch nails between his fingers!

But Geoff and Barry never thrilled me like one chap of fifty years ago did with feats of strength bordering on lunacy. I was the *Yorkshire Evening Post*'s tame reviewer of shows at the City Varieties and the Empire, Leeds, for forty-eight memorable months before King George VI called me from my burgeoning newspaper career to fight for our country.

All the music halls included speciality acts to complement the top-of-the-bill act. And it was a successful formula, with many and varied performers, like high-speed acrobats who hurtled into a series of supple flip-flops, and jugglers who balanced precariously on huge balls and propelled them up and down sloping boards. We had novelty routines like the French chap — who was probably born in Batley — swallowing live fish, snails, nails and razor-blades, and regurgitating the lot into a tank. His *piece-de-resistance* saw him push live frogs down his throat and he would announce in nasal tones borrowed from Maurice Chevalier:

'Zey are trez bon, how you say enchanting, and so varry, varry deleeecious.'

We had another crackpot who was a high-wire man with a difference. His trick was to stand on his head on the cable which was suspended from the gallery down to the stage. He paraded in tights and had a cushioned cap on his curls. Attached to the snappy headgear was a grooved wheel. And he placed this on the wire to help him speed in a death-defying slide to safety. The drums rolled and his lovely assistant, in fishnet tights and basque, paraded her long limbs and pranced round the stage as she waited for our hero to make his headlong return.

But they — and hundreds of similar turns — had nothing on my favourite strongman, who had the appearance of a shaven-headed Prussian with moustache drooping at the side of his unsmiling lips. He always summoned a few likely lads from the audience and equipped them with sledgehammers. He then bent his body into the crab-like shape of a one-man rugby scrum, balanced paving stones on his chest, and allowed the eager volunteers to smash them into smithereens.

Henry Vaddon was his name. And he was a star even though he never topped the bill. His act built up to an incredible climax. There was a lady helper who fired a huge iron ball at Henry's midriff. It boomed from a cannon which exploded clouds of smoke as it despatched a sphere capable of punching a hole through the *Ark Royal* in the direction of intrepid Henry.

But he saved the best until the last few seconds of his spectacular contribution to the world of entertainment. Henry placed a First World War German helmet on his head. It had a spike on top, and this played a part of paramount importance in the ultimate trial of strength. When Henry was happy with his headgear, he would start to spin a heavy, iron-bound, full-sized cartwheel, complete with spokes and brass centrepiece. It was fairly fizzing within a minute as it revolved round his fist and gathered momentum. Henry would then hurl it sky-high and allow it to land with a zonk on the spike. You always knew when the trick had worked. Henry's neck almost disappeared in his shoulders. His eyes creased like a chap with constipation. He shuddered, turned crimson and invariably released an asthmatic gasp of 'Hellfire!'

Henry was a tower of strength, a colossus, a man of immense build, with the type of Charles Atlas physique spoiled only by a rapidly shortening neck. But his cry of 'Hellfire' still lives with me. It is probably my favourite Famous Last Word.

All the 'Fun' of the Fair

He wrapped his lips round the pint of liquid sunshine, drank deeply and told everyone in earshot:

'I'm with the feast. Experienced on waltzers and dodgems. That's me. There's none better.'

The lofty qualification was proclaimed with the justifiable pride of an academic who had learned of his honours degree. And why not? It is not given to everyone to tread roaring fairground monsters, sporting a totally nonchalant countenance, sliding on and off the thundering roundabout with the grace of Nureyev, and collecting fares at the same time. It is a knack, a gift, and gains the admiration of less nimble mortals who stand in silent envy of the slick romeos — who, if not exactly ladykillers, have the panache to wound a few.

Feasts — or fairs as the nobs knew them — were one of the exciting features of our childhood. We had them at all points Yorkshire. They were magnetic attractions, providing fun for all the family. They were a dream world for starry and often sleepy-eyed tots. They spawned trials of strength, skill and courage for young bucks, flexing muscles and fluttering their metaphorical plumage to attract and impress the shy and simpering opposite gender.

Did you ever swing the hammer in an attempt to send a block screaming up a post to ring the bell at the top? Did you try to stick a trio of separate playing cards with darts, or peer down the bent sights of a pop-gun rifle, having placed the 'ammo' — like tiny arrows with tufted flights — into the barrel? I remember the chap who created mayhem when he shot everything in sight. He sprayed his 'ammo' into bowls, vases, plates, dollies and ducks. The owner of the shooting gallery dived for cover. He emerged and trembled as he surveyed the damage. And he heard the delighted youth demand his prize.

'Give me one of those clay pipes', he hollered.

Thumping sounds beating from steam organs battled with discordant record music blaring from the waltzer and dodgems. And, when an extra-big drum and king-sized cymbal joined the cacophony, the banging and crashing heralded something special.

'Roll up my bonny lads', shouted Professor Bosco, promoter of the boxing and wrestling booths, and a man gifted in barking dialogue designed to stir lads from the village into challenging squash-nosed, ear-chewed, hulking pugilists. They were usually called 'Kid' and they niffed of Fiery Jack embrocation, sweat and stale Hammonds pale ale.

'Are you men or boys?' taunted the professor. 'Surely we have one among you who can go three rounds with my man for a fiver?'

A fiver indeed! It was a king's ransom. It was a crock of gold. It was a tantilising, tempting but jolly elusive prize. Few — if any — finished the encounter with clear eyes and the ability to adopt an upright stance as the strident bell signalled the end of the final round. The majority of the game novices ended with legs as limp as bootlaces, puffed eyes threatening to take on a multi-coloured hue, and a wan smile which begged: 'Rescue me please from this sporting lunacy'.

What happened in the clinches was nobody's business. The over-adventurous challenger would quickly have the peepers he trained on that fiver closed by a gouging thumb. And head-butting, standing on toes, the occasional bite, and a flurry of low-blows and kidney punches were all part of the booth boxer's armoury. Of course, he did it without the referee noticing. And the ref was usually Mario Magisti, who summoned the protagonists to the centre of the ring and growled:

'I want a fair fight, and the more blood I see the more I like it.'

Mario always held up his hands which were minus a few fingers. He claimed that he had them bitten off when he wrestled in Madison Square Garden, and we believed every word of his fantasy.

After Mario's stint as ref, he would slip into swimming trunks for his reappearance as a grunting grappler to tackle such 'goodies' as the Farmer's Boy, or pit his fouling expertise against the likes of Cockney Knight or Ed Blondie Gordon.

Another tent housed the world's smallest circus, with a tiny pony called Rosie — or was that the name of the twelve-stone beauty who sparkled with the sequins sewn on her abbreviated black costume? The tiny pony counted up to six by pawing the ground, and the lady wobbled her voluminous attractions across a tight wire placed at least a foot above the sawdust base of the ring. After her death-defying act, she would stand at a board to have her dad hurl knives at her from a distance all of three feet. And then she sold popcorn, and took her turn at lambasting the drum which told us that the circus had come to town and that another performance was imminent.

Wrong End of the Stick

Two elderly ladies talked over a cuppa in a Wetherby tea shop, and one said: 'When I first married...' The other old dear interrupted with the remark: 'My goodness. How many times have you been married?'

Judging by the scandalised expression on the face of the once-wed pensioner, her companion had got the wrong end of the stick — as we old fogies are apt to do.

It happened to Joe's missus Bertha the other day, and he was not a bit pleased about his wife's reaction to one of his party tricks. Joe is knocking on. He has certainly reached his biblical allocation of three score years and ten. But you wouldn't believe it. He has a spring in his step, a twinkle in his bright blue eyes, and he will definitely see a few more out before he becomes a candidate for what he terms 'a wooden overcoat'. Joe attributes his rude health and jaunty gait to his formative days. He waxes lyrical when he talks about his childhood. He almost drools when he recalls home cooking, breadcakes cooling on the back-door step, and rabbit pies. His eyes go misty when he talks of a horde of brothers and sisters.

But I wonder if Joe is as nimble and agile or as well as he claims? Are cracks beginning to appear in his veneer of bursting vitality? Is Joe coming apart at the seams?

The other day Joe walked out of the bathroom and he dropped his discarded shirt in the direction of one of those straw washing baskets. He calls it an alabaster but I believe he means Ali Baba. However, the shirt missed and it lay in a crumpled heap at the side of the Ali-watsit. Joe decided to perform a trick he often did in his younger days. Instead of stooping to pick it up, he toe-ended the shirt into the air and grabbed it with his hand before placing it in the receptacle. Joe's wife Bertha noticed this acrobatic action. But she did not appreciate that he was simply recapturing — for a brief second — the nifty footwork and supple flexibility of his youth. Bertha was not impressed. She turned away from her loved one. She shook her head, produced a couple of tut-tuts, and declared:

'Poor Joe. You're getting old. You can't even bend down nowadays.'

Joe was incensed. He denied that there was anything wrong with him. He attempted to touch his toes and he suddenly realised that his 'kicking' leg hurt like billyo. And if you have never had a pain as acute as billyo, you have never suffered. There was only one thing Joe could do. He went to our medical centre — the place one of the doctors left to go back on the buses — and he saw the replacement healer, who asked kindly: 'What's the trouble?'

Joe rubbed the affected part of his right leg and said: 'I have a pain here.'

'It's your age', the doc replied.

'My left leg is just as old', Joe persisted, 'and it doesn't hurt.'

He left the surgery clutching his prescription. He arrived home with a jar of pills, a spray, elastic bandages and a worried frown. But Bertha had the appropriate cure — a strong cuppa, and a good natter round the kitchen table. Joe recalled:

'I always used Fiery Jack and Sloans Liniment when I had an ache or a pain. But I had an unfortunate mishap with Sloans. I splashed some on my chest — like Henry Cooper did in that advert — and I used too much. It ran down and I won't tell you where it finished. But it gave me gyp for an hour or two.

My mother had all sorts of remedies. She used to treat a sore throat by wrapping a sweaty sock round it. I don't know what magical properties they had, but she swore by them. Mind you, I always preferred one of my own socks — not our Jack's. His would have done more damage than good. When we had colds, we used to stick our feet in mustard baths. We also had mustard plasters. In fact the only thing we didn't have mustard on was our meat, because we rarely had such luxuries as a joint of beef. We were more the stew type of family. I can't count the number of times I had a bread poultice stuck on my chest and, of course, onions cured everything. If I came home with a broken leg, you could bet your last ha'penny my mother would boil onions in milk. What with sweaty socks, sulphur, mustard and onions, we were not exactly nice to know. It's little wonder we were called a close family. Nobody else came within yards of us.

But I remember when my mother ran out of remedies. I had
a stiff shoulder and a bad back, and even onions failed, so I
was sent to see the Hully Gully man out Denby Dale way. I
paid him half-a-crown and he approached me from the back.
He grabbed me in a half-Nelson, jerked my head one way and
my shoulder in the opposite direction. There was a crack and
a sudden stab of pain, and I was back to my old self. My
stiffness disappeared. My back was brilliant. But the following
day I felt a bit uncomfortable. I went to the public dispensary
and waited for hours. It was then diagnosed that I had a
dislocated collarbone. The Hully Gully man cured two of my
complaints but gave me another. By jingo I was sore.'

Joe finished his rambling. He drained his pot of tea. He
rose slowly and tenderly from his chair. He expected stabbing
pains. But there was nothing — simply that God-given feeling
of get-up-and-go. Joe nearly broke into a dance.

'It's a blooming miracle', he said. 'It must be the cuppa.'

He embarked on another bout of recapitulation. He turned
to me and murmured: 'Do you know when I was first
married ...'

'How many times have you been wed Joe?' Bertha interrupted. 'Is there something you're not telling me?'

Snap-happy Days at Geoffreys

'You're as pretty as a picture...' warbled the crooner on the car radio, and I was immediately launched on yet another nostalgic trip down Memory Lane. It wasn't the singer's pleasant tones or his enunciation. In fact his 'picture' sounded more like 'pitcher'. But the phrase conjured scenes of doting mums and aunties taking children of varying shapes and temperaments to the photographers ... usually Geoffreys.

Do you remember this emporium of photographic creativity? Geoffreys was on Boar Lane, Leeds, where reluctant and often recalcitrant kiddies were dragged screaming and kicking by parents who simply had to fill another page in the family album. The various stages of growing up were faithfully captured by a chap who dived under a cover, peered at the upside-down subject, hollered 'smile please' and squeezed a button to produce yet another happy, happy snap.

Junior's first visit to Geoffreys was made as soon as the unsuspecting babe was able to adopt an upright pose. He or she would be stripped as naked as the day they were born, plonked on a cushion, and — to their everlasting torment — photographed in the wherewithal. The picture would be shown to granny, auntie and even strangers, who dutifully cooed their admiration of the little nipper minus nappie. The same audience would later turn spotty teenagers into bundles of squirming embarrassment with the nudge-nudge, wink-wink remark: 'I've seen a photo of you in the nuddie'.

I recall with vivid clarity two occasions when I was almost bound and gagged to get me to Geoffreys. But there was an irresistible bribe, a palatable temptation, a firm promise of a treat from my Aunt Eliza.

'Be a good boy, sit still and smile at Geoffreys, and I'll buy you fish and chips at Youngmans. We won't have them standing up. We will sit down in the upstairs cafe', was her pledge. And it would have taken a child with more stern resolve than I had to refuse such an offer.

But there was a price to pay. Can you imagine having your hair brushed into a rolling kiss curl? Can you contemplate the agony of an estate kid having to put on a white satin shirt, tailored grey jacket, short trousers, ankle socks and the type

of shoes Shirley Temple wore when she sang 'On The Good Ship Lollipop'? But I endured the ignominy and I braved the taunts of my scathing compatriots. I withstood the unwarranted slur on my tough-guy exterior — simply because Youngmans beckoned.

The second visit to Geoffreys took place a few years later when I was converted from ordinary mortal to devout altar boy, and it was ordained that I would be pictured for posterity in my cassock and surplice. The war dragged on. Material for clothes — even for religious purposes — was in short supply. But my Aunt Eliza was never short of inspiration, and a roll of Black Italian — diverted from its intended purpose of becoming black-out curtains — miraculously arrived at our house. It was probably bought on the black market. My cassock was made. My surplice was a cut-down version of one discarded by the parish priest, and I remember waiting for my turn in Geoffreys.

One man wound a half-Nelson grip on an infant who lashed out with fists and feet in protest against photography. The perspiring cameraman held a stuffed toy aloft, whistled, clucked and pleaded in vain with the struggling babe to 'watch the birdie'. It took three adults to hold another child. They knelt behind with their hands stuck up the back of the tiny tot's frock to keep her in an upright posture. They were like a ventriloquist working a doll. And she screamed blue murder. Eventually the photo was taken, and no doubt the end-product gave the impression that one of Reuben's angelic cherubs had been snapped by our man at Geoffreys.

Then it was my turn. With eyes raised to Heaven and hands joined in pious supplication, I posed — like the insufferable little prig I must have been — for the photograph which delighted our nearest and dearest. But I admit now, I did it all for the alluring delights of Youngmans who — in those days — served the finest fish and chips known to man.

My future could have been with Youngmans, because my mother's cousin Bill Wimble was Frank Youngman's partner in the shop which opened in upper Briggate near the Headrow, Leeds. But, true to family tradition, my distant relative pulled out of the project, saying 'Fish-and-chip shops will never prosper'. Mr Wimble, in his wisdom, opted for a garage interest in Batley, leaving Mr Youngman to make his fortune.

I became a connoisseur of fish and chips. Those sold at Youngmans — upstairs or down — were like manna, the food of the gods. It became my haunt, especially when I had a night reporting job, and it was there I made the acquaintance of a hypnotist and pyschologist from Filey. I sat at his table, and it must have been obvious to him that I was not at one with the world. I was a picture of misery. He asked me the reason and I blurted out that a boss at the *Evening Post* was giving me a hard time.

The stranger said: 'Describe him.'

'He is a pompous, fat, short-legged, bad-tempered, little so-and-so', I replied.

And my newly acquired counsellor recommended: 'Next time he picks on you, have a mental photograph of him without his clothes on. Picture him as a naked baby on a rug at the photographer's. That will put him in perspective.'

It did, too. The next time the gaffer gave me an undeserved rollicking, I dissolved into a fit of giggles and, believe me, our relationship improved from that moment of mirth.

Offally Scrumptious Treats

What's so awful about offal? I ask the question because of a conversation I had with a couple of teenagers in one of those plastic emporiums where fast food is the house speciality. There was nothing wrong with their thick half-pounders, bag of matchstick chips or cartons of fizzy drinks. But I would swap the lot for a pig's trotter, a pound of vinegar-marinaded tripe or a finger-sticky portion of cow-heel.

'Uuggh' grimaced a young diner when I mentioned the succulent fare of my childhood.

And she echoed the reaction of the vast majority that register face-pulling disgust at the mere mention of those Northern delicacies. Black puddings and sheep's head are rich in minerals and vitamins. But ask any youngsters to sample them, and they would label you a Borgia and swear that you were trying to bring their youthful lives to a premature and poisonous end.

Time was when market places had stalls crammed with tripe and trotters. You could buy trunnel pies and peas, cover them with lashings of vinegar, pepper and rich gravy, and scoff the piping plateful in the open air. I fairly drool at the memory. Even the peas tasted different in those days. They were boiled into a seasoned mush, having been steeped overnight with a block of carbonate of soda to bring the dried morsels to an edible softness.

Offal provided delicious eating between the wars, simply because North-country folk could not afford to buy more expensive meat. And don't forget that Yorkshire puddings were usually served first to take the edge off hearty appetites and save on the main course — if the household budget stretched to an entrée.

I must admit that offal is scarce on the Morgan Menu, and some of the palatable items I have mentioned are non-existent and will never have the benefit of the Lovely Maureen's culinary art. She draws the line at anything she considers to be more gruesome than liver or kidneys, and I have to live on my memories when it comes to tripe and trotters.

I took the Lovely Maureen out for a meal in a seedy cafe the other day. It is the sort of place you can eat dirt cheap. I asked for a T-bone. And the waiter replied: 'It will be thirty pence. With meat, £12.50.'

There was a table menu with the offer 'The Chef's Special'. A wag had pencilled underneath: 'The waitress is quite nice, too'. But the grubby list of fare also included the tempting item: 'Rabbit stew and dumplings'. It was too good to miss, and I can honestly say that I have never slurped a tastier meat-packed broth or devoured, with an appetite bordering on ravenous gluttony, more fluffy suet dumplings. I almost hollered for seconds.

I have been in some filthy 'caffs' in my time. Reporters are not proud. And I remember one in Leeds where a wall notice warned: 'No two people to eat off one plate'. That was the lowest of the low. But the curries served in this establishment were simply and honestly ecstatic if one ignored the grime and grease clinging to chairs, tables, 'curtains' and the proprietor. It is amazing how such places can produce a gastronomic feast fit to fill the tummy of the most discerning gourmet.

I remember a Yorkshire epicurean called Tom talking with glowing rapture of dumplings. His pink features beamed. His eyes gleamed as he developed his theme of dumplings. He was in poetic mood. He described them as 'round and big as footballs and as bewitching as the smile on the face of a lovesick maiden'. But Tom also had his disappointments. He recalled:

'Me dad and me had been in t' canteen for us dinners. When we came ahrt I said to me father: "Her dumplings were a bit sad, dad." Me dad almost cried: "Sad, me lad. Sad ... they were ruddy heartbroken!'

We are proud of our Northern food. And why not? People below Watford Gap are apt to scoff at our produce instead of scoffing it. But those who wrinkle noses and pretend to go faint at the mere mention of tripe will cheerfully accept the snails, horse-meat, beasts' tongues and cow-heel, yes cow-heel, placed before them by continental restaurateurs. It would appear that offal is acceptable in Paris. But naff when it comes to home consumption.

Such good food became a joke for music-hall comedians and Cockney comics who sang numbers like 'Boiled Beef and

Carrots' and usually spent the rest of their half-minute act taking the Michael out of our trotters, not to mention our clogs and cloth caps. Jokes like: 'I went to the doctor with my liver — he gave me a pound of onions', made audiences fall about. But not me.

I am looking to the day when someone will have the courage and commonsense to open a tripe-and-onion emporium with trotters, cow-heel and black puddings dominating the bill of fare. The menu would claim in gold-leaf letters 'Under Distinguished Patronage', and underneath the proprietor could pen 'Purveyors of quality offal to the aristocracy', and give the unique and much-needed establishment another touch of Northern class. Or is that all pie in the sky … preferably trunnel or offal pie? Because there is nothing awful about offal.

Don't Mention the War

Helmut was a welcome little visitor to the happy Morgan homestead when we lived in a rather posh detached house. The German lad soon settled and he ate well. In fact I have never seen a child with such a gross appetite. He could, as they say, eat one more tatie than a pig, and he used to demolish colossal meals, almost lick his plate, and he was first in the queue for seconds. Yorkshire puddings were much to his liking. He gazed at them, took a deep breath and ploughed into the fluffy titbits with great gusto. The sparks fairly flew from his 'irons'.

Helmut's mother must have been aware of his eating ability, because she made sure that her darling offspring would not go hungry. After every meal Helmut clicked his heels, bowed to the Lovely Maureen and retired to his bedroom, where he ate black bread which his mother had the foresight to cram into his suitcase. He brought half a dozen loaves with him, and we found most of them under the bed after he had returned to the Fatherland.

Helmut came to us on an exchange visit. One of my lads lodged with his family in Hamburg, and we looked forward to Helmut making a reciprocal trip and joining us for a fortnight's stay in Yorkshire. But — being the head of the family, and mindful of the mischievous ways of my recalcitrant trio of lads, as well as being conscious of Helmut's feelings — I delivered the dire warning:

'Do not embarrass our lodger. Do not say anything out of place. And do not mention the war!'

A few days after Helmut's arrival, I returned from work to hear animated chatter coming from the drawing room (more swank). I could detect the staccato burst of machine-gun fire and the angry buzz of aircraft. And I charged into the audience of lads watching a film. You have probably guessed that it was *The Battle of Britain*. The viewers roared every time a Jerry plane hit the deck. And Helmut cheered louder than the others during the scene when tomato-coloured gore splashed from a German pilot before his plane spiralled into a smoking dive of death. Helmut jumped to his feet and yelled admiration of the sharp-shooting Spitfire ace.

I thought of that cameo when the *Yorkshire Evening Post* promoted a night of poignant nostalgia. It was an occasion when we remembered the few to whom so many owed so much. We dressed for the part. Old uniforms came out of mothballs. We danced to the music of all those years ago. We sang *Bless 'em All* (the clean version), we joined in the chorus of *The Siegfried Line* and we chanted to the rabbit to run, run, run. We talked of Pascha cigarettes, dried egg, ration books, gas masks and air raids.

We had an Anderson air-raid shelter which was the envy of the neighbourhood. It had more flowers on top of it than you would find in Kew Gardens. It was wall-papered. It had bunk beds, an electric light and a heater. It was the last word in shelters. But we could never get in. The neighbours always beat us in the mad scramble, and we all know that possession is all-powerful even in the legal world. We were reduced to 'camping' under the sturdy front-room table. And my Aunt Eliza and my mother Norah held their rosary beads and implored every saint in Heaven to guide and watch over the world and especially their nearest and dearest.

Thankfully we all survived to tell the tale. And by golly we did tell it at our evening of nostalgia. So many blessings were counted and so many silent prayers were offered for those who made the supreme sacrifice during the days described by

Winston Churchill as 'The time when Britain found its soul'. We had to laugh when we talked about evacuees, and we heard one particularly entertaining story about Lady Pembroke, who filled her stately home with children and was amazed to discover that one tiny urchin had never slept on a bed.

'We kids sleep under the bed', the laddie explained. 'Beds are for dead people and we aren't ready to be laid out yet.'

Over 830,000 children were taken from their homes and billeted with other families, and 103,000 teachers travelled with their pupils as they listened to Vera Lynn singing 'We'll meet again'. The evacuees probably joined in with more hope than confidence. But we made the rafters ring when we sang the same tearjerker at the end of the Battle of Britain festivities.

As we left, we gazed at the 'bomber's moon'. Our reverie was interrupted by a wag who broke the spell with an innocent observation.

'If the bloke in charge of the navy is called the First Sea Lord', he murmured, 'I wonder why the chap who is boss of the army is not called the First Landlord? And what's more' he added, 'the man who governs the Royal Air Force should be given the title Lord Of The Flies.'

It was that kind of silly humour which enabled my generation — and the one before — to survive the Battle Of Britain and win it.

I wonder how little Helmut — now big Helmut — is? I must drop him a line sometime.

Have you Been?

The outdoor collection provided the income from which cathedrals, churches and schools were built. And I was barely out of short trousers when I was entrusted with a Sunday morning round to receive threepenny bits, tanners and the occasional bob.

It was a simple enough chore, and most people responded to my door knocking with a cheerful greeting, even though the giving of the 'widow's mite' often strained the family's limited resources. There were houses where children joined in the chorus 'Shintin'. This conveyed that the lady of the house was probably hiding behind the curtains, and that her purse and budget were probably in parlous straits. There were other homesteads where it was as well to gain the trust and friendship of the family mongrel. And there was one where it was prudent to ignore the question asked by a well-meaning pensioner, Mrs Degnan. She usually greeted callers with the query: 'Have you been?'

I was naive, and the first time she asked I shook my head to signify 'no'. As the day progressed I wished that I had hollered 'Yes'. She invited me into the kitchen, reached for a bottle and poured out a decent measure of Californian Syrup of Figs. 'Open wide', she commanded, and the sweet, treacly concoction was spooned down my throat. Within the hour I had 'been'. And in another ten minutes I had 'been' again.

It transpired that Mrs Degnan — like so many silver-haired old grannies — had a fixation with the internal plumbing

system. She believed in keeping family, friends and even casual visitors 'regular'. She had great faith in purgatives.

There was a spinster, Sarah Feeley, who offered visitors cups of a tea-like brew called Monastery Herbs. It was an acquired taste, and if the monks drank copious amounts of this beverage they certainly did their penance on earth.

It was not a patch on senna pods, which were also highly recommended by Mrs Degnan. They were often brewed and drunk in our house when one family member or another 'had not been' for a day or two.

We were never short of All-Fours, Cab Driver's Linctus, Fennings Fever Cure, Carter's Little Liver Pills, Lung Healers. Scotts Emulsion, Doctor Payne's Pink Pills for Pale People and Cod Liver Oil. We had the inevitable bottle of California Syrup of Figs and chocolate-covered laxatives. And there was also a mixture of morphine and arrowroot, which had the reverse effect — a boon to people who 'had been' too often.

There was a chap at the back of Leeds Market with many lotions. One was an embrocation which he actually drank and claimed: 'If it is good for my inside, it is good for your outside'.

He also sold castor oil, which was probably the most popular antidote for constipation, and also came in handy for removing the squeak from door hinges and lubricating bike chains. I once applied it to my crowning glory when my pocket did not stretch to proprietary brands of hair-dressing. But it was not as good a substitute as liquid paraffin, which also came to the aid of folk who 'had not been'.

We had virol and malt at school, and one of our nuns was known to dole out Californian Syrup of Figs to needy recipients. She also professed deep faith in the power of brimstone and treacle. But I don't know if this was administered to pupils who 'had been' or who had not.

I thought about the good sister and also called to mind Mrs Degnan at the weekend because I don't think my so-called high-fibre diet contains enough roughage. It is not having the desired effect. It probably calls for more drastic action — like the tried and trusted remedy of a king-size dose of Californian Syrup of Figs.

By the way — have *you* been?

Pennies from Heaven

The story is told of Charlie who became a gasman and collected money from domestic meters. He did the job for a month, but abruptly disappeared from the scene.

'We've been worried about you', another gas board employee informed him. 'There are four weeks' wages waiting at the depot.'

Charlie gasped: 'Do we get paid as well?'

The tale came to mind when I thought about the stream of door-to-door cash collectors. Many knocked with more hope than confidence, and regularly drew the response: 'Me mam says she isn't in'. This holler from behind a firmly latched door conveyed to the luckless caller that the lady of the house was not available and that the family purse was as empty as Old Mother Hubbard's cupboard.

But the gasman usually gained entrance. He was a popular visitor, and I was reminded of this by my old friend and retired radio raconteur Tim Heley. When we were children, the appearance of the gasman often resulted in a timely 'windfall' in the shape of a cash rebate.

You recognised the gasman. He wore navy-blue trousers which were shiny at the kneecaps from kneeling to read meters. He had matching jacket, a peaked cap, and he carried a little brown leather bag — like the one the doctor or midwife used.

'I was one of six children', Tim recalls, 'and we would bound into the house shouting "Mam, t' gasman's in t' street", and our mother would clear the well-scrubbed kitchen table. When he knocked, we crowded round to watch him take his key to the back of the penny-in-the-slot meter, turn it and bring out the coin-box. He emptied the pennies on the table, and he always grinned as we bent over to get a sniff of the money, which reeked of coal-gas.'

Tim's gasman had a pocketful of blue paper bags and he counted what we called 'clods' into piles of twelve. Then he would put five bobsworth into each bag and pop them in his hold-all. Our gasman had sheaves of stiff brown paper. He wrapped this tightly round rolls of coins. He folded the ends, which were given a sharp bang to make them secure.

Like Tim's chap, our man would do a mysterious sum. He totted the figures, licked the point of a stub of pencil and entered his findings in a long black book. It had a broad elastic band — like a garter — to hold the pages together. Tim remembers:

'When he finished comparing the amount of cash with the gas consumption, there was always a few coppers over and these were handed to my mother. If there was more than a shilling we usually got a penny apiece for the sweet shop. It was always a highlight when the gasman came.'

We had gas-mantles when I lived as a child in Castleford. When they flickered and the room darkened, it was a broad hint that the light-giving vapours were about to expire. Pennies were required. I remember running to our local grocery shop to change a shilling into pennies and racing back in time to keep the mantle aflame.

One of our neighbours had no such problems. He boasted that he maintained a constant supply by plugging into the street gas-lamp nearest to his house. This claim was never verified, but I do remember a bobby arriving one day to lock him up.

Here Comes the Tingelary Man

I saw one the other day — a tingelary. It was not in mint condition. In fact it was downright dilapidated. It had definitely seen better days. But there was no mistaking this instrument of musical magic. It was, indeed, a tingelary.

The woodwork, shafts and wheels were rickety and in sore need of restoration. And so was the shabby Liverpudlian who hauled the relic of the lean years round the streets near Aintree racecourse. But the creaking machine, and its equally well-worn attendant, still produced a certain sound of music. It was loud and rhythmic. It was rich and velvety, and it entered the soul.

It turned back the clock six decades, when children — and often fortified grown-ups — jigged in the streets whenever this melodious wonder-of-the-age came into view.

The tingelary man was usually of Italian extraction and sometimes he was accompanied by a playful monkey. Its job was to hold out a tin for people to pop in ha'pennies, a 'threepenny Johnny' or even a silver 'tanner'. The tiny creature sported a red fez and embroidered jacket. He had a small bell tinkling from his collar, to which a long thin chain was attached. This allowed him to leave his perch on the tingelary and romp with the excited audience. But it also prevented any idea the monkey might entertain of escape.

Leeds had a strong community of immigrant Italians who quickly integrated and brought a colourful presence into many a drab existence. They introduced us to the tingelary, the barrel organ and the monkey, and who will ever forget the cry of 'Hokey Pokey, penny a lump'? That is how the Italian ice-cream sellers announced their arrival in the vicinity. They pulled their gaily painted barrows, and served cornets, twists and sandwiches from a freezer stuck in the centre of the distinctive conveyance. They hollered 'Hokey Pokey — penny a lump'. And we responded with: 'It's just the stuff to make you jump'. This was because of the freezing touch on the tongue. If you swallowed a mouthful too quickly, the sides of your temple throbbed and ached with the sudden shock. It was ice-cream to lick, savour and roll round the palate. It was not a delicacy to bolt in chunks.

Why the name 'Hokey Pokey', you might well ask? My Italian friends tell me it was a corruption of 'Ecco pocco', which the ice-cream vendor shouted to announce that he would be 'here for a little time'. But children quickly adapted 'Ecco pocco' to 'Hokey Pokey'.

But back to the tingelary. It apparently derives its name from tingal-tangal which, the *Oxford Dictionary* explains, was some kind of musical soirée often held in places with doubtful reputations.

Mr Tomasso was our tingelary man. His family produced renowned musicians like Freddie and Ernie Tomasso, who played for Harry Gold and his Pieces Of Eight, among other great bands. But old Mr Tomasso's musical love was the tingelary, which he hauled for countless miles to bring an inimitable brand of entertainment to kids on the block.

I had many Italian friends. I was reared with the Friola, Capitano and Lusardi families. They worshipped at St Nicholas's Church on the Gipton Estate in Leeds, and their joy was always in evidence when the visiting priest was Father Ronchetti. It was then the older Italians, and the good priest, conversed in their native tongue. It was a mystifying experience for me, but I did pick up one exciteable expression, and that was 'si si', which they appeared to use in great abundance. I often responded with 'si si' when Father Ronchetti asked me a question. And, in doing so, I probably replied 'yes yes' when I should have been saying 'no no'.

The Lusardi family traded under the name Granelli. They manufactured 'Hokey Pokey', and also owned a cafe in Leeds Market where they made the best Spam sandwiches it was possible to buy throughout the war years.

Saturday morning was a ritual. I shopped for my mother at Liptons, where customers made an attempt not to have their ration books stamped so they could nip next door to Gallons and double the family's weekly allocation of wartime grub. It did not happen every weekend but, when it did, the mid-morning break for a breadcake filled with Spam became a celebratory banquet. I used to perch on a high stool at Granelli's and wait for Winnie Connor to do the serving — because she was most generous with the Spam. After the 'sarnie', she served up a banana-flavoured milkshake, which produced a suitable end to another triumphant shopping expedition.

The 1920s saw poverty-stricken days of mass unemploy-ment, the General Strike, and an era of austerity and anxiety. The 1930s were not much better with the threat of war. And the 1940s resulted in heartbreak and agony for those who ached for the safe return of loved ones from various scenes of hostility and carnage. But there were many moments for childish delight in hot summer months when Hokey Pokey merchants and Mr Tomasso — the man with the tingelary — came into view. It was a precious part of our upbringing.

Calls of the Past

I took a stroll round the Calls in Leeds, and 'By shots!'— as my old boss Bill White used to say — the place has changed.

Years ago the Calls was not exactly a salubrious spot. It bordered on the smelly riverside which had Penfold and Rank warehouses in dominant positions. It overlooked a rat-infested wharf which was used as a car park and was not always safe to be — especially on a foggy night. The Calls is now a posh residential area with luxurious riverside flats nestling at the side of impressive office blocks, expensive hotels and restaurants. But it was not always so inviting.

There was one point in my journalistic life when I paid daily visits to the Corn Exchange and Leeds Market to collect items of information. And I often bumped into 'knights of the road' who congregated in the Calls for a morning session of 'Spare a copper for a cuppa, governor'.

Some slept rough, with sacks and newspapers providing modest insulation. Other bedraggled beggars were choosier, and elected to sleep in the warmth of brick kilns in Meadow Lane before the early morning sortie to the Calls for a spell of 'tapping'. You did not have to be a member of the CID to detect those who had opted for a kip in the kilns. They emerged covered from tip to toe in red brick-dust which rose in clouds from their tattered clobber and lingered for hours after they had taken their leave from their dry but dirty digs.

Many of them used to traipse from the Calls to Mount St Mary's Convent, where they queued for a pot of tea and mound of dripping and bread. The life-giving sustenance was handed through a grille by the good sisters, who had a dedicated regular in a chap with the nickname 'Apple Harry'. He was a member of the 'brick brigade', and kids used to run a mile when he came into view. More timid children — like me — ran two miles because he invariably grabbed the wrists of anyone who fell for his offer: 'Do you want an apple, kid?' The story went round that 'Apple Harry' grabbed out of personal fright because he believed children were about to attack him. We were assured that it was not a menacing gesture on his part. But few of us were inclined to put the theory to the acid test.

The Calls had a couple of pubs which attracted what my old mother called 'floosies' or 'ladies of the night'. There was a bookmakers' shop owned by the city's first lady bookie, Edith Statman, and there was a tiny shop which sold pop, crisps, sweets and sandwiches made by a motherly soul, Mrs Barron. She always placed an extra slice of ham and beetroot in the breadcakes when I ordered and I think I was one of her favourites. The Calls was a base from where Wallace Arnold buses and Heaps Tours departed and returned passengers from day trips and longer holidays. And the nearby River Aire had a bridge from where you could watch elongated barges carrying all manner of cargoes up and down the polluted waterway.

When I think of barges I recall Alf Hawkridge, who was a cashier at the *Yorkshire Evening Post* by day and a comedian called Al Kilham at night. He used to tell the tale of the tramp who approached a bargee on the River Aire towpath and asked: 'Can I work my passage to Manchester'. The skipper replied: 'Aye, tha can lad. Get odd of yon 'osse's head'. He did too.

The jokes never change, do they? But — by shots — the Calls and surrounding district have.

The Splendour of Rummaging

Isn't rummaging a great word? It describes to perfection a frantic scramble, the sort of thing ladies do when they attack a pile of clothing at a jumble sale — and exactly my mode of operation when faced with a pile of books.

I love to rummage through dusty volumes. I can't resist literary bargains on trestle tables outside bookshops. I spend hours leafing through pages of publications which have prices like one shilling and sixpence printed on the front cover.

One of the more quaint purveyors of the written word is a chap who runs an equally quaint public house at Stalybridge Station on the railway line leading from Leeds to Liverpool. I had a portion of his famed and tasty pie and black-eyed peas the other day, and also rummaged through the books he sells for charity. I emerged triumphant with a paperbacked racing novel written by one of my boyhood heroes, Nat Gould. The original price was one shilling. I secured it for five pence. It is in mint condition and must be a collector's item.

Nat Gould's plots never changed. He discovered a winning format and he saw no reason to experiment with new ideas. The simple books were good sellers and in great demand by lads and ladies alike. Only the names of the characters differed, and this must have been the most demanding job for Nat, who had to dream up suitable titles for his heroes and villains. The storylines always included an impoverished but good-living racehorse trainer, who had a beautiful daughter who owned an equally charming filly. Daddy's stables were usually mortgaged to a wealthy rascal of an owner, who would force his unwanted attentions on the trainer's fair and slender offspring. But she inevitably spurned his evil approaches, because she was already in love with a handsome jockey. The moustached villain was usually behind a scheme to 'nobble' the talented nag, who represented the only chance of restoring the family's dwindling financial fortunes. The malicious plan invariably misfired, leaving the almost human thoroughbred to escape from the capture and malevolent intentions of the nefarious gang. Then in would move the elegant and handsome rider to partner the filly to short-head victory and save the day, daughter, trainer's yard, and restore the old man's money and reputation.

I haven't read my new-found and treasured Nat Gould yet. But I am prepared to bet my bottom dollar that the précis of the yarn is not far off. And I wouldn't want it any different.

Nat Gould used to lose all his hard-earned money to the bookies, and return to his study to pen another tome for his ever-ready publisher and eager public. The more renowned author Edgar Wallace had a similar affliction. He gambled away thousands of pounds, but always had a book in the pipeline to earn enough cash to settle his Turf debts.

I recently rummaged in a shop in Helmsley, where I picked up a tattered cookery book which was obviously once the property of a lady who worked in kitchens for the nobility. I marvelled at the apparent gross appetites and digestive powers of those who who sat down to devour half a pig stuffed with pheasant guinea-fowl, mutton, pigeon and beef.

I also read the chronicles of a Yorkshire sage who reported the story of a man who was devastated when his beautiful wife went to meet her maker. The widower mourned her passing. He was grief-stricken and distraught. He pined for his loved one and he bought a marble gravestone to her memory. It was erected at the head of the grave, and he commissioned a gifted stone-mason to chisel the immortal phrase:

'The Light Of My Life Has Gone Out.'

Shortly after his loss, he met a new sweetheart. He courted her with charm and courtesy. He proposed. She accepted, and they were married. He told his newly acquired bride of the tombstone and she asked to see it. When they arrived hand-in-hand at the cemetery, they gazed at the inscription, which the new husband had wisely altered and now told the world:

'The Light Of My Life Has Gone Out — But Since Then I Have Struck Another Match.'

But when it comes to real rummaging, I am a complete novice. I had to go to a charity bring-and-buy sale and drop in a cargo of unwanted bric-a-brac at a school hall. It was there I saw a professional rummager in action. One lady of ample proportions tore into a scrum like a rugby forward. Shoulders and elbows gained her a front row position, and her flashing fingers retained and rejected items with the speed of light. She is a record-breaking rummager and an education. And her husband approved her skill — and robust frame — as he watched her with justifiable pride and undoubted admiration. He stood at the back of the hall and one could almost hear him murmur:

'I love every acre of her. She is a wizard.'

The lady asked for prices. She blanched and dropped any article rated at more than fifty pence, but she emerged from the mountain of clobber clutching a mound of goodies to her hefty and heaving bosom. She pounded the pile into her surprised but still smiling hubby's outstretched arms, sucked in a deep breath, and returned to the battle with renewed energy and enthusiasm.

Her ringed hands were like the cranes you operate with a penny in seaside amusements. They have claw-like grabs on the end of a string. You drop them on to objects and turn a wheel to close the iron fingers. But the champion rummager was dealing without the wheeling. She has brought rummaging to an art form, and I envied her knack and know-how if not her manners.

Rummaging is a splendid pastime. And it is a great word, isn't it?

A Light-fingered Touch

There is a chap in our local called Barry who, it is whispered, 'has a bit of form'. Barry is the type of furtive chap who speaks from the corner of his mouth, gives you a knowing dig in the ribs, and can get you anything at rock-bottom price. He dresses like the original comedy wideboy, Arthur English, and is never short of a merry quip, ending every sentence with 'You know what I mean'.

Barry was what we used to term a 'juvenile delinquent', and now known as an innocent product of problem parents with marital hang-ups. His penchant for pinching started at a very early age. And his mum was concerned about his shoplifting and bedroom cache of acquired goodies. When this glittering and ever-increasing haul started to match Aladdin's Cave, she took him to a psychiatrist. The good doctor talked to the youngster for hours and eventually diagnosed the problem. He told the worried mother:

'It's quite simple really. Barry is a thief.'

But are we all inveterate nickers of other people's property? My mate Jim always stirs his coffee with one of the fistful of office-issue ball-point pens he regularly brings home. He has been known to chortle:

'Some people will pinch owt. Even my wife had her face lifted.'

We have another neighbour whose son was asked what his father did at work. The lad replied:

'He makes light bulbs and toilet rolls. That's all he ever brings home.'

And that innocent confession came to mind recently when I bumped into an old pal, George Firth. George has retired and lives in Bridlington. But there was a time when he was mine host at the Viaduct, Lower Briggate, Leeds. We yarned about the old days, and George recalled that one of his customers was a market trader, who was invariably first through the door at opening time. George and his regular always made small talk, and then the landlord — remembering that the following day was Mothering Sunday — asked the market man if he would bring in a potted plant when he called for his evening pint. The chap duly obliged. He arrived with the blooming foliage, placed it on the bar, and said to George:

'Take it with my compliments.'

Another customer overheard the act of generosity and asked: 'Can you get me one?'

'Where do you work?' the trader responded.

The chap replied: 'The Royal Ordnance Factory, Barnbow.' Quick as a flash the plant purveyor asked: 'Can you get me a tank?'

If you cast your mind back to the war years, you will remember that thousands of cigarette lighters were in circulation and all were manufactured by lads and lasses who worked at the Vickers aircraft factory, Blackburns or Barnbow. The lighters were oblong with a wheel on top. This sparked a flint held in position by a tiny spring, and the barrel contained cotton wool which you impregnated with petrol poured through a tiny screw-hole in the base. Cartridge cases — with the rifle bullet removed — were also turned into lighters, and I once returned one to a hawker with the complaint that it was not working properly. He quickly exchanged it for another, and gave me the stock answer for the failure of the fag igniter to function:

'The spirit is willing but the flash is weak'.

The lighters were, of course, made from armament spare bits. And it would not have surprised me had an aeroplane or two disappeared on to the black market from Blackburns' factory at Gledhow Wood, Leeds.

But my favourite act of small-time larceny occurred in the famous Whitelocks hostelry in Turks Head Yard, Briggate, Leeds. I was almost an eyewitness to a 'heist' which embarrassed the Leeds City Police Force, and baffled the full team of Criminal Investigation Department detectives.

Bobbies were out in force for a party. The celebrated bar was packed with wall-to-wall coppers. A huge side of roast beef was paraded on an equally large silver platter and it was placed on the bar in preparation for carving. It was ready for the making of the pub's famous sandwiches, spread with dripping, and filled with thick portions of meat and as many pickles as a customer could plaster between the generously cut slices of bread.

The officers of the law sank pints of Number 3. Conversation flowed. And then it was time for the grub. A hush descended on the gathering. The beef — and the salver — had disappeared. The bobbies giggled and mused: 'This is a practical joke'. They shouted: 'Come on, own up. Who has hidden the beef?'

There was no answer. And suddenly the sordid truth began to dawn. Constables were confused. Sergeants were subdued. Inspectors were incensed. Superintendents were stupified. There were almost 100 sets of police peepers in the pub. And the beef had been stolen before their very eyes. Headlines blazed the embarrassing news. There was a general hue and cry. The nefarious incident almost demanded fingerprints and tracker dogs. But the miscreant — obviously a well-fed one — was never apprehended. The policeman's lot was not a happy one that night, and I bet the criminal still has a laugh about the time when he or she cased the joint … and the platter.

'Yes, times is bad', agreed Barry, as he sipped his G-and-T in the pub last night. 'It's hard to make an honest living. You know what I mean. By the way', he added, 'do you know how I can get rid of 140 shoes? Unfortunately they are all for left feet. They fell off the back of a lorry. And I've been done. You know what I mean!'

Stitched up the Hard Way

Time was when we took our various aches and pains to the doctor's surgery and sat in a waiting room gazing in stone-faced silence at similarly afflicted folk. We wiled away the tedium with mental guesses at what sort of ailment might be troubling the grey-haired cove sighing in the corner, the flustered mother with a trio of nippers clutching her skirt, or the young lady with a suspicious bulge under her coat. You cast surreptitious glances at her clasped hands, trying to spot a wedding ring, and, when you tired of this vain pursuit, you yawned and reached out to a knee-high table to pick up a magazine. Dozens of piercing eyes followed this action. And your hand hovered momentarily over *John Bull*, *Picture Post* and *Titbits*, only to settle on a fading and boring geographical publication with a boring feature about hulking hippos wallowing in a muddy habitat. The only time the assembled patients broke into animated conversation was when one or another queried their place in the queue.

'Am I before or after you?' one would whisper with red-faced embarrassment.

That was the signal for an outbreak of agitated murmuring, with all and sundry identifying their position in the line-up.

But the return to a funereal atmosphere was inevitable, with the ticking of a Potts clock, the rippling of magazine pages and an occasional yell from one of the skirt-clutching kiddies to break the sound of silence.

We have six doctors at our centre. (We did have seven, but one went back on the buses.) It is quite luxurious, pleasant and civilised, to the extent that we have piped music playing softly in the background to soothe the twitches of anxiety.

A friend of mine fulfilled her appointment the other day. She perched on the sofa. She idly turned over the pages of a glossy mag, and she was captivated by the tinkling beauty of a piano concerto emanating from the loudspeakers. She said:

'The glorious sound filled the room. I closed my eyes and drifted. Suddenly I was jerked from my reverie. An elderly lady at the side of me shuffled her feet. She kept looking at her watch and clicking her tongue with tut-tutting annoyance. I asked her what was wrong. The pensioner replied: "I am baby-sitting for my daughter and have to be there in a quarter of an hour. My appointment was for twenty minutes ago and I got here on time. I am sure the doctor knows he is keeping me waiting. But he is not bothered. All he wants to do is sit in his surgery and drive us crackers playing that ruddy piano."'

We didn't have musical recitals in Doctor Belton's sparsely furnished chambers on Burley Road, Leeds. The Irish-born medic did not play the piano. But he did play pop with philanderers who called in to be 'thrown on the sick'. When patients asked for something to make them sweat, he signed them off. He always claimed this drew more beads of perspiration from their bodies than a mustard plaster or a hot toddy.

I once had to make an unscheduled call on the good doctor's services after the Lovely Maureen had pressed me into a bout of do-it-yourself. She asked me to prise a piece of wood from a pane of glass. And I performed the task at the expense of a lacerated finger which extracted the hysterical scream 'I'm bleeding to death!'.

I bound the wound in a towel and dashed to Doctor Belton's waiting room. I jumped the queue of outraged patients and burst into the surgery, where I dripped more blood than you saw in *Quo Vadis*. The alarmed doctor was more concerned about his floor than my injury. But he decided to stitch the damage as he issued the warning:

'God help me. But it's a long time since I did anything as surgical as this.'

Doctor Belton fished out a curved and ancient needle. He pulled from a drawer an equally antiquated Bunsen burner with a wick sticking from the purple spirit. He used a full box of Swan Vestas to light the apparatus, and then he stuck in the needle in interests of sterilisation. Everyone knows that metal is a conductor of heat — except the doctor — and the white-hot needle kept burning his fingers and extracting a yell of anguish from the scorched surgeon. He constantly dropped it on the floor, which necessitated another session of sterilising and another bout of pain. Meanwhile I leaked another couple of pints of gore on the surgery floor.

Doctor Belton tired of the smell of roasting fingers. He decided to commence stitching without further ado. But he lacked the skill of a cross-legged tailor. He squinted through his spectacles, sucked the end of the catgut, and attempted to thread it through the needle eye. He cursed as he missed by the proverbial mile, and we had to combine forces to finish the job. He held the still-warm implement with his burnt digits and I pushed the catgut through the tiny cavity.

Doctor Belton then began operations. He cringed and so did I when he aimed the blunt point at my finger and, after a few wild stabs, he pierced the sides of the gash and pulled a length of catgut through. He whooped joy and satisfaction. But his elation was short-lived. We searched his desk, drawers and big leather bag, but failed to find a pair of scissors to cut what he termed 'The blessed, damned, useless, vile lump of cotton'. We settled for a strip of sticking plaster ... yards of it. And Doctor Belton was just as adept at wrapping elastoplast round my poorly finger as he was at stitching it.

I finished up with a mound of broad plaster wrapped round and round my hand and wrist. It stretched up to my elbow because Doctor Belton had to keep winding until he exhausted the roll. You see — he had no means of cutting it.

Such an entertaining diversion — or crisis — could not happen in ultra-modern medical centres. And I must admit that I rather like them.

Getting to Grips with Technology

You must have seen those American films based on hard-bitten reporters yelling into stand-up telephones, the receiver lodged between their ear and collarbone, and a cigarette drooping from the corner of their mouths. They wear snap-brimmed trilbies — even inside the office — and when they hurtle to an assignment, they turn up the collar of their shabby raincoats with an air of careless abandon. Their editor is always a balding and invariably bad-tempered bourbon-supping scruff with a green eye-shade. This chap never goes home, and he constantly reaches for stomach pills because the job of shouting 'Hold the front page' goes cap-in-hand with persistent ulcers and griping wind.

But the scene in the modern reportorial emporiums of most British newspapers is more decent, dignified and in keeping with our deserved title of 'Gentlemen of the Press'. And the era of the eye-shade disappeared with the passing of the pigeon method of sending despatches from one source to another. Not that I do not remember such days and aids.

I recall the time when our bosses were cussed old codgers with fiery tempers, snuff-stained waistcoats and nicotine-flecked moustaches. And they wore starched dickies and stiff collars attached with studs to the neck of their union-twill shirts. Many sported a spotted bow-tie, which made some of them look as though they had dropped from the arm of a musical-hall ventriloquist. And they pulled on a hard hat and black coat in winter — or straw boater and linen jacket in summer — before setting sail for their daily visit to one hostelry or several.

The call to alcohol was always signalled at one o'clock sharp. I think a bell rang in their heads. And they left the office as grumpy gaffers without as much as a word of fond farewell, and returned after two hours mellow and, to all intents and purposes, entirely different men. They glowed and gazed at we mere mortals with glassy eyes. They had a more relaxed approach to what was left of the working day and they smiled indulgently on lesser lights who pounded with two flashing fingers the yellowing keys of Barlock or Imperial typewriters.

Today we use computer terminals — electronic marvels which defy the comprehension of such dullards as yours truly. It has taken me almost three years to assimilate the basics of this baffling wizardry, and I know how utterly mystified most people must have been when the cat's whisker wireless gave way to battery-operated radio receivers.

I can also imagine how our newspaper predecessors felt when the pigeon method of sending copy — which was still in operation when I first started work at the Yorkshire Conservative Newspaper Company Ltd — was superseded by the dit-dah-dit sound of the morse code system. Outside our wire-room were pigeon lofts which once housed the feathered 'employees'. Elderly telegraphists often talked about the times they had to tempt the homing bird to land with the lure of a handful of corn scattered on the ground. The tale was also regularly told of the copy boy — usually a man of near-pensionable age, but still responding to 'boy' — who finally grabbed a bird after it had made repeated efforts to avoid capture. The 'boy' was asked for the message from the pigeon and he warbled: 'Coo, coo, coo'.

But times have changed. Or have they? I thought about the old days when our news editor — half the age of a 'boy' — hollered to one of his staff: 'Be a dear and pop downstairs to interview a chap who has just completed a tour of the world.'

The instruction jogged memories of the day I penned copious notes about a newly married couple who lacked nothing when it came to the spirit of adventure. They decided that they were in danger of stagnating in their respective jobs and, to their eternal credit, they opted for circling the universe. They pooled their money, bought a van, and we wished them *au revoir* as they embarked on their round-the-world challenge. The story and pictures appeared in full. We faithfully captured in print and photography the tears of those left behind, and — though I say it myself — it was rather a nice job. And I duly raised my titfer in salute as the happy pioneers set off on their palatable journey.

A week later I walked through Leeds and accidentally bumped into a young girl. And I found myself apologising to the lass who had made the headlines. She blushed and stammered:

'We had a tiff and only got as far as Doncaster. We are back home.'

Did I dash back to the office to swallow my embarrassment and write a follow-up story? You're darned right. I didn't.

I still feel a crimson hue on my cheeks when I contemplate that incident, as I do when I think back to the time when a group of journalists enjoyed our annual Father's Day trip to Blackpool. On the return journey, we called in a pub near Skipton to sample a lethal cocktail which had been specially prepared for us by the landlord. It was passable. But we weaklings decided that it was too strong for our delicate palates and we dispensed pints of it to elderly pub regulars, who expressed gratitude for our kindly offer. They didn't the following day. They couldn't. Our fiery drink had nearly wiped out the village's complement of pensioners. In fact two of them were in the intensive care unit at the local hospital, struggling for survival. Happily they did. But we did not report the scoop story, although it is fair to assume those gum-chewing, fag puffing, word-drawling stars of American newspaper movies would.

We are now firmly entrenched in the magical world of new technology. But stories don't change and neither do people. You will still find folk in this materialistic age with hearts as big and soft as the proverbial boiled turnip. You might even find a journalist with the same tender quality.

Yorkshire Invaded

It was a miserable weekend at Morgan Manor the day we learned that a long-established Yorkshire cricket tradition had been clean bowled, leaving many of us stumped. The Lovely Maureen's Yorkshires — usually risen and fluffy — flopped like crêpe soles. They were in sympathy with those who believed that our county cricket hierarchy should have adhered to the acclaimed custom of picking players born within the boundary of the Broad Acres.

Many still mourn the change in attitude, and will never recover from the initial shock of learning that 'outsiders' would be selected to represent our proud county in the cricketing arena. Bert in the local summed up our feelings at the Sunday lunchtime session which closely resembled the official opening of the Gloom Club. He hardly touched his ale, and that is not like him. Bert can usually see his first pint off with one sip and two gulps. But he toyed with his beer. He looked out of sorts. And he growled:

'We want none of yon foreigners. I wouldn't even let one pull the roller.'

Time was when Yorkshire cricket ruled the world. It reigned supreme at county level. And we were proud of our sporting religion. We didn't play the game. We 'laiked' and loved it in the days before our heritage was split asunder. We became the laughing stock of the cricketing universe simply because we hadn't the sense we were born with. We 'weshed' our mucky laundry in public during the protracted Boycott business, which divided committe members and fans alike into separate camps. And our rivals fell about as we squirmed with self-inflicted embarrassment. The only item of self-respect left was our 'Yorkshire only' tradition. And we were stripped of that last vestige of saving grace the day we changed the rules.

When I was a lad we couldn't wait for the cricket season to start. Every street was a Test-match arena. Every available wall had stumps and bails chalked on it. Balls did not have leather cases. They were 'corkies' with a ridged seam and they quickly lost their coat of red paint. They were lethal missiles in the hands of Johnny 'Titch' Rourke and Andy Cunningham.

They were mates who hurled them with scant regard for the safety of lads whose only protection was a roughly hewn bat.

Do you remember those home-made bats? I had one cut and shaped from paling broken from a dilapidated fence. When it connected with the corky ball, a thousand electric shocks shot up the arm. Your hands — and brain, if any — went numb. And they stayed that way until life returned with a bout of tingling pins and needles. Few lads lasted more than one over, and my monstrosity of a bat finished its days sailing down the local beck.

I recall Stanley Liversedge arriving in the neighbourhood. He had a proper sprung bat, and he also wore a cricket cap because he was in a team at the high school. 'Titch' Rourke used to do his utmost to knock Stanley's cap off, and he often succeeded with bouncers and beamers which threatened decapitation. Objections to this intimidation brought from 'Titch' the far from comforting grunt:

'You've got a bat in your hand, haven't you?'

Stanley's bat was a prized possession and jealously guarded. If he wanted to be 'Len Hutton', he bagged the name without opposition. If he wanted to open the batting or bowling, his requests were granted simply because he might take his bat home and our 'laiking' would come to an abrupt end.

Cricket has always been worshipped in the county. We rejoiced in Yorkshire's dominance of the county scene. We lacked nowt in confidence and we held the firm belief that, when Yorkshire was strong, England had few worries.

Our cricketing tales became folklore. I remember the Bradford League club signing a bowler for £75 with the promise of another £75 if he took 100 wickets. By the time he had collected ninety-eight, the team had won the league title and the cup, so he was not asked to bowl again and £75 was saved. We remember the tale of Emmott Robinson sinking to his knees before a Roses Game and praying:

'Lord, if thee wants Lancashire to win, they will do. And if thee wants Yorkshire to win, we will. But if thee can keep out of the way for the next three days, we'll knock the stuffing out of 'em.'

I recall with delight the years I worked at the side of former England and Yorkshire bowler Bill Bowes, who often chuckled to himself when he reflected on his experiences. He told of the day when he asked Emmott if he had ever suffered injuries and the bowler recalling:

'I did the hat-trick against Sussex and I had two broken ribs. But you didn't tell anyone, because if you didn't laik, you didn't get paid.'

Bill never tired of the story of a collier who was summoned to join the Yorkshire team because one member was injured.

'The lad turned up straight from a night shift', Bill said, 'but he was washed and changed, and he attended a pre-match party at the Savoy in London. The new boy insisted on paying for a round of beer and he plonked £1 on the waiter's tray. When he returned with the drinks there was only eighteen pence in change, and the man — eager for a tip — murmured: "Remember the waiter, sir".

"Remember you?" the player thundered. "I'll never ruddy forget you."

Cricket historian Harry East always claimed: 'No atheist ever became a good player'. And that is probably because the game — we tend to believe — was fashioned in heaven, with the edict 'Yorkshiremen only in the Yorkshire side'. But when you come to think of it, the 'outsiders' we admitted have not done a bad job, have they?

Sounds from the Fifties

I am sure the ghosts of Hetty King, George Formby, Eric Morecambe and Ernie Wise, Albert Whelan and many more theatrical spirits emerged from the fading plaster at the time-honoured City Varieties just to see what a few hundred elderly 'teenagers' were up to. We were there to turn back the clock to the fabulous fifties and that never-to-be-forgotten era when ballad singers entertained and entranced those young enough to enjoy *Juke Box Jury* and *Six-Five Special*.

You must remember Craig Douglas of the baby-face looks, slim figure and lilting larynx. Nearly forty years have elapsed since he appeared at the Ace of Clubs, Leeds, which was only one of many 'watering holes' for tired journalists. And, after four nightly excursions to that fun palace, we knew Craig's act backwards and we decided to help him out. Craig appealed for hush and told the packed house:

'If the gentlemen of the press don't mind, I will sing the next number without assistance.'

Craig admits that he is now growing a see-through patch on his once curl-covered cranium and he is facially a little plumper. But he can still pull on 'flared' pants made in 1960, and the pipes are still clean and clear.

'I had several hits', Craig said, 'notably in the Hebrides, Mongolia and other far-flung places.'

Craig achieved a lifetime ambition by appearing at the City Varieties. He said:

'It is a lovely feeling to be able to claim that I have "trod these famous boards" and I would like to thank a lot of people. I thank my mother and father for making all this possible in the first place. And my five children for making it essential. If you have enjoyed the show, tell your friends. If you haven't, this theatre is the London Palladium and my name is Des O'Connor.'

Our hands were sore as we clapped a greeting to a shy, retiring Ruby Murray who had to be propelled to the microphone because she had terrible stage fright. Ruby once had five songs in the top ten at the same time. And even the Beatles failed to manage this claim to vocal fame. (Sadly Ruby died in 1999, but still singing to the end.)

'Let's get one thing straight', Ruby croaked. 'I am not full of cold. I don't have a sore throat. This is my normal voice. I'm afraid that when I was a baby my mother left me out in the rain and I rusted up. I know you will all be wondering if I will make the high notes. I am terrified too that I won't.'

But she did, as did the top of the bill performer, man with umpteen years experience, a master of his art, and still as fresh and barnstorming as he was in the days when he recorded twenty-seven hits. Ronnie Hilton told us of his four Royal Command performances and how he met the Queen after the concerts.

'She was wonderful to me', he said. 'And so was her husband, Prince Albert.'

We joined him in 'I Still Believe', 'Veni Vidi Vici', 'A Blossom Fell', and many other eternal favourites, including the song about the Amsterdam mouse. Ronnie informed us that the little creature is now thirty-six years old.

'I am fed up of singing about him' he added, 'but I wish I could find another song like it tomorrow.'

You don't need a new one, Ronnie. You still have us, the oldest teenagers in captivity. I am sure the ghosts of Hetty King and all the rest enjoyed it just as much as we did.

That Sinking Feeling

'In the swim' is an expression known only too well to such former Olympic champions as Adrian Moorhouse. But it strikes terror in the palpitating heart of lesser mortals like your land-loving scribe. I believe in diving in the drink. But only to quench a raging thirst. And — as the world's worst swimmer — I will never be considered for the job of bookie's runner in Venice.

There was a lad who was taught to swim at a very early age by his dad. He found it quite easy after he had escaped from the sack. But my introduction to aquatic activities was not so brutal. In fact, my mother was so embarrassingly careful and cosseting, she told me:

'You can't go to the baths until you learn to swim.'

So I spent a couple of years stretched on my stomach across the seat of an upright dining-room chair going through the motions of a simulated breast-stroke and crawl. But the day finally dawned when I sampled the real thing.

I dashed home from school and told my doting parent that our class would attend Union Street Baths the following day. She panicked. Would she ever see her curly-haired cherub again. Would he be lost forever in the cradle of the deep? And what was she to do about getting him swimming trunks at this late hour? Her anxiety about the costume eased. But mine increased, because I arrived at Union Street with a lovely pink bath-towel rolled round a pair of my aunt's white drawers. They were elasticated at the waist and legs but almost invisible against my pale torso. I wasn't too worried when I pulled them up my sparrow legs. They looked like the real thing until I — and they — went under the shower. They became transparent. And I immediately dived for cover, the pink towel, and a quick exit from my introduction to the world of water sport.

The following day my mum went clicking-crazy with her needles. She actually knitted me a swimming costume, and a second visit to Union Street was deemed necessary to try out her handiwork. Have you ever entered a pool in a thigh-hugging garment and emerged with ankle-length trunks? They started to get a bit heavy in the shower. They sank and sagged from the moment I gingerly walked down the steps leading to that always-chlorinated water. And only the good Lord will know how I managed to find the herculean strength to haul myself, and a hundredweight of soggy wool, out of what could have been a watery grave.

The next day, five pals and I paid coppers for admission to Union Street, and for an extra threepence or so hired the right swimming gear. There was only one minor problem. They had run out of junior trunks and we had to take man-sized. But not to worry. Extra tugs on the belt made them fit, and we walked from the balcony — above the cubicles —proudly sporting our pukka trunks with the motif of a leaping swimmer on the legs.

We had an instructor who told us to shower and then jump in the shallow end. He then asked us to grip the bar with palms turned upwards, and with arms and elbows pressed against the wall.

'Kick out your legs and your body will float', he assured us.

Our bodies did. And so did our trunks. They ballooned with water, and drifted down our legs and away from our feet, leaving six eleven-year-old bare bottoms bobbing on the surface.

I did not learn to swim at Union Street Baths. And also made a few abortive efforts at Joseph Street Baths, Hunslet, and York Road Baths, Leeds, where my uncle secured the job of lifeguard. He never informed council officials, who interviewed him for the post, that he could not swim a stroke. They never bothered to ask. So he did not volunteer the information. He looked quite dapper in his fisherman-knit white jumper and fitted trunks. He had a whistle suspended from his collar, and he blew this at the start and finish of every session. He also walked at the side of the bath with a hook on the end of a long pole to fish out any child in difficulties. But he never so much as dipped his toe in the water.

Daredevils used to enter with graceful swallow dives from the balcony, which was used as a gallery for spectators as well as changing quarters. And I envied the courage and ability of those making the intrepid plunge with scant regard for their safety or that of the innocent swimmers floating below.

I always tip-toed down the steps and usually hopped round the shallow part on one leg. My arms did the breast-stroke action, and I occasionally dipped my face in the water and spluttered with great pretence that I was actually swimming. We always finished our visit to the baths with a penny in the Brylcreem dispenser to grease our wet heads. And we indulged in a halfpenny Oxo drink as we wrapped our chilled hands round steaming mugs. I was eleven at the time, and eleven more years elapsed before I actually learned to swim.

My National Service took me to Egypt. We used to bathe and swim in the Great Bitter Lakes. And I always kept close to the shore so that I could safely indulge in my one-legged breaststroke. What I did not know was that the sea bed suddenly dropped about thirty feet. And I walked off the sandy shelf and sank. I still don't know how it happened, but I thrashed my arms and legs about for survival and found myself swimming. It was not stylish. It was not an action from any swimming manual or textbook. But I improved from that near-disastrous moment, and I have been able to swim ever since.

That does not mean I have conquered my fear or dislike of water. When you think of what fish probably get up to, it is enough to turn you off H_2O for good. But — like Adrian Moorhouse — I'm in the swim. Are you?

Not All They Were Cracked up to Be

Eggs are not all they are cracked up to be, and they certainly were not sixty years ago when the first cargo of the dried variety arrived in starving Britain. The yellow powder was billed as 'solid nourishment, easy to ship, cheap to buy', and it was sent to the old country by our American friends who, under a scheme called Lease Lend, helped to replenish our dwindling rations.

In January 1942 a person's weekly allocation of food was eight ounces of fat, including two ounces of butter, eight ounces of sugar, and a meat allowance of one shilling and twopence (seven new pence), of which twopence-worth had to be taken in corned beef. Bread was in good supply, but you were lucky to get two eggs a month, so the dried stuff was a boon.

We had cockerels and hens in plenty during the war years. I remember my father ordering cartons of fluffy chickens from breeders in Hebden Bridge. And I had the job of picking up boxes of the squeaking inmates at Cross Gates railway station and taking them to our smallholding. We fed them on corn and a sprinkling of Karswood poultry spice, and to get our allocation of feed we had to register our egg production with the Ministry of Food. We sent the bulk of the eggs to markets designated by the MOF, which was once described as 'the biggest shop in the world'.

Hit songs in those days included 'Run Rabbit Run' and a rather plaintive ditty which went:

'Hey! Little Hen. When, when, when
Will you lay me an egg for my tea?'

The country's dwindling flock of fowl did their best to answer the plea. But demand exceeded supply and the dried egg came into our shops. The powdered commodity from the good old USA was eyed with grave suspicion by housewives. But the Minister of Food, Lord Woolton, allayed the fears and he pronounced it:

'Fit for human consumption and not a substitute for eggs but a rich source of energy in its own right.'

The nation accepted his assurance, and my mother became a dab hand at whisking dried eggs into a consistency ready for frying, although she had problems when she embarked on more ambitious concoctions. Her dried egg custards had a strange effect on the pastry. The base always floated to the top of the mixture, and we had to eat a type of baked upside-own pudding. Likewise her Yorkshire puddings, which were invariably as thick and springy as crêpe soles, emerged from the oven with the crumbling texture of crispy biscuits. They were one of her few culinary failures, and another was a dried egg crème brûlée, although I must admit you didn't get many of those on our estate.

But the biggest disaster was one experienced by my old pal Mick Dean. Mick often mixed himself an omelette when he returned home from a spell of firewatching with the ARP wardens. One night he reached into his mother's pantry and he picked up a tin in which his mum had inadvertently put Colmans mustard instead of dried egg. Mick added the usual amount of water to the powder and he frantically stirred the mixture, which simply refused to thicken. After a quarter of an hour, he poured the thin concoction into the hot pan and fried the mustard. Mick sampled a huge spoonful. He coughed, spluttered, and breathed fire and brimstone for the rest of the night, with his dear old mum asking: 'Why are you crying?'

It'll be the Death of Me

Just a minute chums. If you are thinking of turning your toes up for the last time and contemplating leaving this mortal coil, hang on for a second or two. The news has filtered through that such an undertaking has increased in price and that it is more expensive to breathe your last than it was at this time twelve months ago. In fact, Jovial Jim — our local laugh-a-minute mortician — has put up his funeral rates by £100, and it also costs infinitely more than it used to do to purchase a plot in God's Garden.

Even our parish priest Canon Shenanigan and his curate Father O'Bubblegum are expecting more for services and their final funereal farewell. They are demanding a few more bob for the undoubted influence they have with St Peter — keeper of the Golden Gates. And it will be in your interests to put another pound or two on the collection plate, because of their close contact with St Peter's omnipotent overseer who will eventually determine your final destination. The good clerics are nearer to God than thee and — like seaside landladies — they have to live when you are gone. So make sure that you don't hang back when it comes to crossing the priestly palm with silver. It is rumoured that Old Nick is having a sale of bedsits. But Hades is hellish and far too hot at this time of the year, so if an increased stipend — and a few

more charitable turns on your part — can open the portals to Paradise, then pay up with a smile and behave like a good 'un.

But I can tell you now pals — if the costs continue to soar then I am not going. It is as simple as that. Dying is becoming too expensive a pastime. Soon only the wealthy few will be able to afford a deathbed scene for a tearful goodbye.

I am reminded of a rather poverty-stricken household in the Emerald Isle where villagers visited the Murphys' home to pay their respects. They trooped upstairs to the sparsely furnished bedroom where Murphy's remains lay on the wooden floor. The mourners looked in vain for a bed on which to rest their departed friend, and one suggested that the coffin should be supported on a set of chairs. It was Eamonn who shouted to the family assembled downstairs:

'Send up three chairs for Murphy.'

And Murphy's kith and kin roared: 'Hip, hip, hooray. Hip, hip, hooray...'

Of course newspapers can add to the spiralling death duties. You have to pay to advertise your passing. But it is doubtful if there is a more widely read column than the Births, Marriages and Deaths section, and you may have noticed that readers are ultra co-operative and are born, wedded and die in alphabetical order. This daily service is a compelling read for the majority of our customers, and is sometimes known as Hatches, Matches and Dispatches. But a colleague once came up with a new description which never caught on, and I'm not surprised. He labelled the column 'Yells, Bells and Knells'.

I remember the name Ada Hardcastle appearing in the list of deceased, and she had quite a send-off. In fact her husband Alfred talks about it to this day. Alfred booked the Jovial Jim, whose ancient hearse doubles as a mini-bus during the cricket season, and he told the funeral director to spare no expense and make sure everyone enjoyed themselves.

I often talk to Jim in the local. He might do me a cut-price job one day. When business is not as brisk as it might be, he murmurs:

'We could do with a sudden frost or a nice bout of fog to boost trade. But I suppose we will have to be patient and wait for the winter harvest.'

He is that type of philosophical chap. He can be relied on to wear the right sort of miserable face throughout official proceedings, and he always insists on protocol and putting people in their right places when it comes to cars and cortège. I remember he turned to Alfred and said:

'Will you sit with Mrs Davidson?'

And I recall Alfred's reply.

'I most certainly will not', he barked. 'She's my mother-in-law and sharing a cab with her will spoil my day.'

But Jim is a kindly and understanding man. He fawns on his drivers and coffin-carriers, and gives them a new peaked cap apiece every five years or so. Rumour has it that he once bought a job lot from a chap who worked for London North Eastern Railway, or was it the LMS? It doesn't matter. But he does have the welfare of his staff at heart, and when he heard that Joe Hesletine was in danger of joining his maker, he made a mad dash to the bedside.

Joe is a mountain of a man. He always does justice to his wife's cooking, and people from far and wide murmur admiration of a chap who is renowned for his expertise with a knife and fork. Little wonder that he tips the scales at twenty stones or more.

The undertaker was rightly alarmed. Joe looked like Mount Vesuvius under his eiderdown. He even belched and dropped ash, and it was obvious to our Jim that there would be a weighty problem when the invalid was ready for his last procession.

'Joe, please consider my men', Jim pleaded. 'They are not big lads like you. And there is a fair distance to cover from the church to the graveside. The terrain is a bit rough and rocky. And my lads will have to carry your coffin on their shoulders. Do you think you could do a bit of dieting before you say ta-ta? Can you pine a bit and cut down on the calories? Consider my lads if you will. They might strain themselves.'

Joe didn't lose weight. But he did the next best thing. He decided to recover, and he is still with us, telling the tale, puffing his pipe and enjoying his pint.

I have decided to join him. There's no point in going because, to put it bluntly, I simply can't afford it. I'll just bury myself in my work. Cheers.

Fortune Goes up in Smoke

Are you a collector? Are you one of those people who hoard the most useless items of bric-a-brac? Are you frightened to throw anything away? I must admit that I am one who is always reluctant to part with rubbish and make the excuse 'It might come in useful one day'.

It probably stems from my childhood when 'collecting' was all the rage. We stored corkers, beer mats, marbles and train numbers. We had stamp albums and swapped our spares. And we had literally hundreds of cigarette cards.

Do you remember the various series ? They were endless, with jockeys, footballers, exotic birds, racehorses, film stars, wild animals ... the lot. Cigarette packets like Wills Wild Woodbines, Kensitas, Craven A, Robins and of course Senior Service, Capstan and Players all had an assortment of cards, and you were the envy of the other kids when you completed a full set of fifty pictures, round which you stretched a tight elastic band. You see cigarette cards mounted and framed these days, and they cost the earth. And I often wonder why I did not save the many packs I had as a child.

I was reminded of the collecting pastime when a club comic told the tale of the chap who was mean and always refused to offer friends a fag.

'The last time he opened his cigarette packet', he said, 'a picture of Stanley Matthews dropped out.'

And it also revived memories for one of my acquaintances of the days when he had a mammoth collection of cig cards, birds eggs and beer bottle tops. He said:

'I used to collect all manner of things, and every Monday morning, on my way to school, I used to rummage in the bins outside the local working men's club. I searched for empty cigarette packets because it was odds-on that the cards would still be inside. It wasn't every smoker who valued them. My only trouble was that the club steward had two great danes on a long chain. And you had to be alert to keep out of their way. One day I was digging in the bin and I spotted a card I required to complete a soccer set. I was so excited, I didn't hear the dogs coming. Suddenly they were snapping at my heels. I dived in the adjoining bin, putting the lid on behind me, and I wasn't rescued until dinnertime when the steward arrived to open up the club. "I've warned you about messing about in my bins', he shouted. "Come out you little so-and-so." "Never mind about me", I cried. "Tommy Lawton is in the other bin." "Good God!" he hollered, because he actually thought the centre forward had sought shelter in the dustbin. He was very disappointed when he realised that I meant a picture card of the famous player.'

My pal's beer-bottle-top collecting was a popular pastime. They had a thin circle of cork in the cap, and you took this out, stuck the top on the outside of your jersey and placed the cork disc inside to make the 'badge' stick.

'On Mondays I always wore Websters beer bottle tops', he explained. 'On Tuesdays I would change them for Ramsdens. But the headmaster forbade me to wear them after an incident with a lady teacher. She was leaning over me to correct my spelling when she got a whiff of one of my Tetley Pale Ale "badges". She nearly passed out, and rumour had it that she was taken home quite light-headed.'

I was never enamoured with collecting birds' eggs. It was a messy job making a hole in both ends and blowing out the contents. But the pride of my friend's collection was a 'golden eagle's egg'. His father brought it home and told his offspring:

'The golden eagle nested on the top of our boiler house and this is her egg.'

The youngster was the star of the neighbourhood. His mates were wild with jealousy, and eventually one of them saved up £5 to buy the rare specimen. The deal was done, but no sooner had my friend pocketed the fiver than the buyer's dad came round to demand it back.

'I can buy a duck egg for a couple of bob any day', he fumed. 'Golden eagle indeed!'

The trouble was that my chum believed everything his dad told him. And so did I.

My father collected racing tips. He had a system which he employed to great success in its infancy and went to London to test it on the Southern circuits. His certain money-making scheme came to an abrupt end when my mother received a telegram from him which read:

'System working well. Please send money.'

He also had a passion for collecting lead soldiers. We had battalions of them, with a full regimental band in bright red tunics and black busbies. I saw a set on the *Antiques Roadshow* and they were valued at hundreds of pounds. Whatever happened to my dad's army?

The Lovely Maureen collects teapots, and she describes me as the biggest refuse collector in Leeds. And that is no way to talk about some of my best friends.

What's in a Word?

Little Johnny was worried. There was no doubt about that. He paused in the middle of sucking sherbet up a thin liquorice tube. His eyes clouded and tears began to well. A frown of anxiety creased his eight year old forehead. Grannie noticed Johnny's apprehension. She wrapped her arm round his shoulders, gave him a comforting cuddle and inquired:

'Whatever is the matter?'

Johnny pointed to a painted notice nailed to a board inside a stretch of dry-walling. It carried the words: 'Cattle for one mile'.

Johnny sobbed: 'I don't know how to cattle.'

You can imagine the innocent lad's feeling of terror. If the warning had read 'cows' or 'bulls', the message would have e been instantly clear. But the description 'cattle' was quite foreign to a diminutive town-dweller who was enjoying a day in the countryside for the first time.

We 'townies' often make unpardonable errors when we pack our cars with kiddies and embark on a day out in God's good fresh air. About forty years ago, I stowed my brood in the family Ford Anglia estate, and we paused at Coverbridge to watch sheep being sheared by an expert who wielded traditional hand-clippers and scorned the electrified variety. He was a lightning snipper. And he ploughed through the flock, removing the fleece and leaving them more naked than the day they were born.

I herded my children and we halted at another field full of the silly-faced creatures, nibbling the grass and apparently waiting for our shearer to pay a visit. I leaned over the wall and shouted over my shoulder to the stragglers:

'Come and have a look at these sheep.'

An urchin of five or six tender years shared my vantage point. He had a dirty face with matching accessories. He was clarted up to the eyebrows and he fixed me with an expression of scorn.

'They bain't be sheep, mister. They be tups', was his stinging rebuke.

The teenty-weeny farmer's boy strode away with disgust written on his grimy features, leaving me to face children who smiled happily at my dearth of knowledge, abysmal ignorance of country lore and my blushing embarrassment. If you have ever been well and truly 'squelched' by an infant, you will know exactly what I mean. I was cowed, or at least sheepish, as I departed from the scene, leaving the tups to the contented cropping of our green and pleasant land.

But back to notices, and people — like Little Johnny — who get hold of the wrong end of the stick in the town and in the country. One of my favourite warnings is: 'Slow racehorses crossing'. I often wonder if this means tortoise-paced nags like those I support at my local bookies.

A story is told about the elderly lady who walked up three flights of stairs at her local department store. She was asked why she hadn't made the climb easier on her elderly legs by taking the escalator.

'There is a sign which says small children and dogs must be carried', said the pensioner. 'And I didn't have a small child or a dog with me, so I used the stairway.'

There was a poster at a zoo in Kirby Misperton, North Yorkshire, and the message was often the cause of consternation. It appears that the management were regularly approached by irate visitors who demanded compensation for articles stolen by the mischievous occupants of the monkey house. The majority of the people had lost their spectacles and failed to retrieve them from the playful animals. One of the zoo attendants was detailed to keep watch on the cage. And he quickly fathomed the reason for the wholesale theft. The monkeys grabbed the glasses when spectators leaned forward to read a small notice attached to the cage. It read:

'Beware! These monkeys steal spectacles.'

The warning was removed, and the nicking of specs ceased forthwith.

Another sign which resulted in major problems was erected just outside Beverley, and the words in bold letters advised, or threatened, 'Fine for Parking'. My pal Ken parked his vehicle and accompanied his wife into the town centre. And they were rather upset when they discovered a plastic envelope on the windscreen with a £25 summons inside. Ken protested that the sign indicated the spot was fine for parking

purposes. But he had to pay, chums, he had to pay. Ken still persists that 'No Parking' means what it says, but 'Fine For Parking' is in danger of misinterpretation.

There is a board on a stake in a field outside Malton and the message reads: 'Please don't throw stones at this sign'. There is another near Grassington which warns: "No Trespassing. Beware Of The Bull. Survivors Please Close The Gate.'

I appreciate messages designed to carry a modicum of inspiration, like the one penned by a boss to his employees. It was exhibited in a prominent position on the office wall and it read: 'This is the tomorrow you worried about yesterday'. One of his pessimistic workers added: 'And now you know why'.

But the notice to beat the lot was the one in the labour ward at the local maternity hospital. It fairly screamed: 'Warning to doctors. Always remember that the first three minutes of life are most dangerous.' A wag scribbled underneath: 'The last three are a bit ruddy dodgy as well'.

At least it makes me cackle. And — like Little Johnny — I would have cattled if I had known how.

The Gentleman of Rhyme

The 1977 Doncaster St Leger was a right royal occasion — the Queen's racehorse Dunfermline was the winner. It was also captured in verse by prolific poet Jack Davies.

Jack first saw the light of day in his native Liverpool. He served for many years as a merchant seaman, and when he bade goodbye to life on the ocean waves he settled in Knaresborough. Jack was a familiar figure on the Northern racing circuit. He sported a bowler, rose in his lapel, watch and chain stretched across his tummy, and he invariably carried a silver-topped walking stick. But sadly he died, leaving us with a wealth of incredible and sometimes unbelievable examples of rhyming poems.

When Dunfermline carried the Queen's racing livery to a memorable victory, Jack could not wait to get home and pen lines in praise of the filly's triumph. Stewards instituted an inquiry into Willie Carson's riding of the winner, but she was allowed to keep the prize, as Jack tells us in his poem:

> 'After a stewards inquiry had been held no interference
>   could be found
> The shouts and cheering was deafening from the
>   crowds that gathered around
> I am sure that in Balmoral those cheers could be heard
> With the aid of an invention by a man named Logie
>   Baird.'

Jack continues:

'Looking in the record books forever will be seen
That a horse named Dunfermline was owned and bred
by the Queen.
"Good Health. Good Luck. Good Racing" what more
can you say
To That Gracious Lady who made history on St Leger
Day.'

You will agree that poets like Jack are few and far between, and he published a booklet with the best of his works included between the pastel-pink covers. Jack had a soft spot for the Yorkshire village of Summerbridge, and he extolled the virtues of this picturesque place with the saga *Where My Rainbow Ends*. Jack writes:

'Somewhere over the rainbow was a song sung long
ago.
When Judy Garland sang it she almost stopped the
show.
If you come to Yorkshire you will climb hills and go
around bends.
To find the little village for it is there my rainbow
ends.'

The poem ends with the memorable verse:

'When it comes to autumn and the leaves are turning
brown
I thank the Lord we found this spot for us to settle
down.
So if you come our Yorkshire way and want to meet
some friends
You will find them in Summerbridge, that's where my
rainbow ends.'

Jack had the happy gift of making friends. I count myself fortunate to be one of them, but unlike Jack's mate Harry Tomlinson I never figured in one of the poet's literary efforts. Jack marked Little Harry's passing with the following:

'It is hard to believe that Harry Tomlinson has gone.
Lived up to the ripe old age of eighty-one
He liked his pint and loved a little bet.
This he told me the first time we met
He was called "Little Harry" by one and all

Many times to his home in Kirkgate I did call.
The very same greeting that he always gave
Was "While you are here will you have a cup of tea".'

Jack was a genius and his talent was not confined to producing palatable poetry. He had the world's largest collection of racing badges — thousands, pinned on a large board which he often erected at sporting exhibitions. He had emblems from racetracks in the Far East, Australia, America, South Africa and from all parts of Europe. He also had shoes from celebrated horses, jockeys' silks and boots, whips and thousands of race cards.

But he will always be remembered and revered for his poetic gifts, and he deserves to rank with the best. To me he was Yorkshire's very own Poet Laureate. His poetry is simple and tells a tale. He didn't baffle readers with airy-fairy stanzas. He painted vivid verbal pictures. When he joined the ranks of pensioners, he told us:

'A full life I have led and now retire
To an old world cottage and a bright red fire.
Hope to make new friends but to keep the old
For the new are silver and the old are gold.'

They are indeed Jack. You had many true companions who admired your work. I keep your little pink book on my bedside table and occasionally read a few of the poems to the Lovely Maureen before we drift into oblivion. I even dreamed that I was writing poetry. But my effort will never match your priceless prose. I wrote:

'Thank you Jack for your book of poems
You will find them in many homes
I read them after we have had our cool drinks
Then we close our eyes for forty winks
We dream and dream of powerful forces
And just like you we love racehorses
My poetic ambitions they rise and rise
Perhaps one day I will win a Nobel Prize
Many thanks to you my dear old Jack
I sing your praise and pat your back
But before I drive you round the bend
This eternal scribbling I had better end.'

The Day War Broke Out, We Laughed with Robb

If there isn't a Robb Wilton Appreciation Society in existence, it is high time there was. And it is as certain as 'the day war broke out' that admirers of the late comedian would clamour for membership.

Robb's name emerged from the crevices of my curly-topped cranium when I rummaged through lumber in a village saleroom and uncovered a dusty and high-domed Cossor wireless. The 'innards' were missing. The valves and mass of wires had long taken leave of the cabinet. But there was no mistaking the object.

We had a battery-operated Cossor at home. We also, at different times, had radios from the Bush, Ecko, HMV and Marconi assembly lines. And I recall the family being the envy of the neighbourhood when my father replaced a wooden model with a set encased in a new-fangled substance called Bakelite.

The wireless played an important role during the war, when the nation crowded round the oft-crackling sets and listened to Winston Churchill's words of pride and patriotism, Lord Haw Haw's morale-shattering propaganda, and the late King's stuttered but stirring speeches of encouragement.

We also had entertainment. Where would we have been without *ITMA* and Tommy Handley's barrage of humour? We had *Happidrome* with Harry Korris singing 'We three. We're not highbrow. Just a set of twerps may be. Ramsbottom, and Enoch, and me.' We had *Bandwagon* with Arthur Askey warbling 'Buzz, buzz, buzz buzz, busy bee, busy bee. Buzz if you like but don't sting me.' And Big Hearted Arthur shared the comedy with Stinker Murdoch and the girl in his life Nausea Bagwash. We had *Hi Gang* with Ben Lyons, Bebe Daniels and Vic 'Hello Lollipops' Oliver. We had *Stand Easy* with Charlie Chester and, of course, we had Vera Lynn, *Music While You Work*, Anne Shelton, *Workers' Playtime* and, best of all, Robb Wilton.

Years after the war I was in Uncle Tom's Cabin, Blackpool, where the cabaret was provided by a trumpet-playing star Nat Gonella. He was on the point of growling his signature tune *Georgia* when he spotted a rotund old gent enjoying a

drink. And he called for a hand-clapping welcome for Robb Wilton — famous for his sketches as Mr Muddlecombe JP, and his skits on the ARP, Home Guard, fire brigade, police and life in general.

Robb was the man who had wartime Britain crying tears of mirth. As Mr Muddlecombe JP he sat on the judicial bench listening to such charges as 'racing tortoises within the thirty-mile-per-hour limit'. He topped the bill on the Moss Empire circuit. When he arrived in Leeds, he was told by an old Yorkshireman: 'Ah've seen them all — George Robey, Wilkie Bard, Little Titch, the lot. None of 'em made me laugh and ah'm sure that you won't.' Within seconds of his act starting, Robb had melted the frigid and cynical critic. He had him clutching his sides, as did the vast audience of listeners who tuned their Cossor radios into his comical characters.

Robb was Liverpool-born straight actor Robert Smith. He was a poorly paid master of melodrama before he discovered his gift for humour. His career changed and he became Mr Muddlecombe, and he later switched to the Home Guard material and the chats he had with the make-believe missus none ever saw. Robb delivered his lines with a degree of slurring hesitation. He clicked his teeth, sucked on his tongue, and embarked on the inevitable opening to his sketches.

Robb said: 'The day war broke out I told the wife, "I've joined the Home Guard and I'm going to stop Hitler and his army".

She said: "Just you?"

I said: "Course not. There's Charlie Evans, Bill Jones ... about seven of us. And we're going to guard the coastline, capture Hitler and stop his troops when he invades."

She said: "Have you ever met this chap Hitler. Do you know what he looks like?"

I said: "Course not. I've never even been in the painting and decorating business."

She said: "How many men will he bring over with him?"

I said: "Thousands and thousands."

She said: "How will you know which one is Hitler?"

Robb — with a lot of clicking and sucking — would pause and then deliver the immortal line: "I've got a tongue in my head haven't I?"

Robb did more than his bit for country and comedy. He was too old to join the forces, but he volunteered for air-raid warden duties. When he completed his nightly music-hall spot, he invariably donned tin hat and armband, and walked round Liverpool ready to pounce on people who flouted the blackout rules and regulations. Robb was frustrated. He had a burning ambition to holler 'Put that light out'. But throughout months of nocturnal sorties, he did not spot as much as a chink of illegal illumination, until one fateful night. A house shone like a beacon. Light poured from every window. Robb climbed over a wall, mounted a rockery, skirted a hedge, rounded a corner, evaded the dustbins and screamed: 'Put that light out!' The order was immediately obeyed. The house was plunged into darkness. Robb could not see a hand in front of him. He had to whisper a timid plea through the letterbox: 'Will you put the lights back on so that I can find my way out?'

He was a one-off. He was an individual. He was an artiste supreme. And he brought our variety theatres — and our Cossor wireless sets — alive for close on sixty years before retiring to Gargrave, the gateway to the Yorkshire Dales.

If there isn't a Robb Wilton Appreciation Society in existence, it is high time there was.

Deadly Ernest

Ernest is not what you would call work-shy. He can look at it all day, and often does. He will never be a bundle of vibrant vitality or nurture a passion for enthusiastic industry. He much prefers loads of leisure and love on the dole.

Ernest has back trouble. He can't get it off the bed. And spasms of pain attack his lumbar region at the mere mention of gainful employment. It is then that Ernest's wife Sally is like a ministering angel. She dotes on Ernest, and declares to all earshot that the problem is both hereditary and incurable.

'It's Ernest's complaint', she sighs. 'It runs in his family. His dad had it and his before him. There's nothing he can do — it must be agony.'

Ernest often wiles away the hours perched on the top step at the front of his house, exchanging the time of day with passing neighbours and strangers. The postman arrived one morning as Ernest sunbathed from his usual vantage spot.

'I feel as though I have walked twenty miles' he said, wiping his perspiring brow. 'My feet are killing me.'

'I'm not surprised', Ernest said. 'Your boots are on the wrong feet.'

'Tha's right, Ernest', the postie replied. 'They should be on thine.'

That remark stung Ernest. It also upset Sally. She sprang with great indignation to Ernest's defence.

'My Ernest didn't dodge the column like some I can mention', she stormed. 'He went down the pit during the war. He brought coal out to keep the munitions factories going.'

'He was only there a day', the postman countered. 'I walked in my mother's coal cellar and brought more out on my boots than he got from the pit.'

It was too much. Sally grabbed Ernest by the collar. She dragged him indoors. She had suffered enough from the jibes about jobs. And she recalled with anger that, only the night before, a bloke in the local club had suggested a suitable present for Ernest of a 'little bone idol'.

'That's the last straw', she thundered. 'I have defended you up to the hilt. You will have to get a proper job and you'll have to keep it.'

'The bookie down the street wants someone to help him straighten out £5 notes', Ernest whimpered. 'I would do a bit of snow clearing but there's none about. And I have always wanted to be a Coronation Day programme seller. But it doesn't look as though the Queen is going to pack in and give me a chance.'

'You lazy good-for-nothing', Sally bridled. 'I'll get you a job if it kills me. You can go and work with my brother at the cemetery.'

Sally was proud of her kin, especially Stan, who was a grave-digger and almost ran the burial front. He was once asked why he had dug a grave far away from the others.

'It's like this', Stan explained. 'The chap who will be put down this hole has nobbut lived round here twelve months and this is where I keep the oddments.'

You can tell he was his own boss and capable of making momentous decisions. And he created a vacancy for Ernest.

'Have him here for seven o'clock tomorrow morning', he told Sally.

Ernest didn't relish the prospect. And he was snoring when the alarm clock almost jumped off the bedside table at six-fifteen. Sally stuck her elbow in his ribs.

'Get up. It's time for work', she said drowsily.

Ernest peered through the windows and murmured: 'I can't go. It's foggy.'

Sally opened her eyes and persisted: 'Don't be silly. I can see over the roof tops.'

'That's not the way to the cemetery', Ernest moaned.

Sally got up. She urged Ernest to stir himself and, to further coax him, asked: 'What do you want for breakfast?'

'Make me a steak and kidney pie', he yawned.

Sally almost hit him with a pillow. She forced him out of the house, and he reluctantly dragged his heels to where Stan waited for him with a king-sized time-piece in his hand.

'Tha's late, but better late than never', said Sally's brother. 'What I want you to do is watch me and you will make a lot of money at this 'ere job.'

After a couple of hour's digging and leaning on shovels, Stan spotted a funeral procession entering the cemetery. The priest conducted the ceremony. The coffin was lowered. And the mourners left, with the exception of one man. Stan moved to his side and murmured:

'I am sure you were close to the deceased. But you can leave everything to me. I will fill in the grave, plant a few flowers, and make it God's tiny little garden. It will be lovely.'

The man turned to Stan and said: 'That's very kind of you. Do you take a drink?'

Stan nodded. And a fiver was thrust into his hand. Ernest watched the routine with a mixture of envy and astonishment. Stan returned to his side and said: 'You know the drill. The next is yours.'

An hour elapsed, and in came a funeral procession. Sure enough, one chap remained after the others had gone. Ernest sidled up and sympathised:

'It's a great shame. I am sure you were close to him. But leave everything to me. I will fill in the grave, plant a few flowers, and make it God's tiny garden. It will be lovely.'

'That's very kind of you', the man said. 'Do you take a drink?'

Ernest nodded. He thrust out his hand for the banknote. The fellow ignored the grasping fist and remarked:

'Well you ought to pack it in. It killed the lad we've just buried.'

So Ernest is unemployed again, and states with 'deadly earnest' that this is how he intends life to remain.

Fetch the Roboleine, I'm Poorly

You must remember the poster which warned us: 'Coughs and sneezes spread diseases, so trap the germs in your handkerchief.' This sound advice came to mind as I dabbed my nose for the thousandth time and incarcerated another million microbes in my mansized tissue.

Streaming red eyes, dry throat, ticklish and irritating cough, throbbing temples and sore nose means only one thing — the dreaded flu. It is not a pleasant experience, and although the world's medical brains have sought a remedy for this annual winter malady, there isn't even a sniff of a certain cure for the common cold, never mind full-blown flu.

Of course patients can be comforted and cosseted with hot toddies, lemon drinks and all manner of patent preparations. But I unearthed a real old-fashioned antidote for colds and coughs in a 1932 copy of the *Yorkshire Evening Post*. The advertisement centres on a product called Roboleine, which is new to me but will probably jog your memory. It was highly recommended for children and adults, and it claimed to 'imbue the muffed-up and miserable with glow and gusto'.

The formula for Roboleine will make current medical experts wince with horror. Have a gander at this, dear reader, and study and mentally digest the ingredients:

'Roboleine is made from marrow extracted from the limbs and ribs of prime oxen to brace pale blood; cream of malt from Scotch barley to pile on muscle; egg yolk to make nerves steady and stubborn; and lemon juice to build healthy bones.'

These were mixed into a product which had a thick, malt-like consistency and cost two bob for a sizeable jar. I can't remember my mother dispensing this treacly substance or even seeing this rather pricey tonic in the house of a posh neighbour who was something of a hypochondriac. This family was so wealthy, they had grapes on display even when none of them was poorly. And I know the lady of the house indulged in a regular tipple of Wincarnis even when she enjoyed robust health. We were on the panel of our local doctor, and my parents must have envied their well-heeled contemporaries who 'went private' and could afford to be 'well-healed'.

But back to Roboleine. Can you imagine what Professor Lacey and our European cousins would say about the contents — particularly the extracts from the ribs of prime oxen?

My mother Norah believed in plain home cooking — we couldn't afford anything else — and she encouraged us to appreciate the nourishing qualities and goodness of oxtail.

'Eat it up', she often said. 'It will warm the cockles of your heart and stick to your ribs like glue.'

I often wondered why my ticker should have 'cockles' and what was the purpose of giving my rib cage a good coating of mucilage. But we believed everything 'our mam' recommended, and we ate oxtail, sheep's head, trotters, scrag-end, spare ribs and all manner of offal with lip-smacking relish and satisfaction. Those were the days when chicken was a rare treat and, like lamb, was a traditional order from the butcher's shop at Eastertide. Chickens were also bought at Christmas by mothers who could not afford the more exotic turkeys, and I will never forget the pride and excitement when my father arrived home with a goose. None of it was wasted, and goose grease was added to the family 'medicine chest'. Did you ever submit to a lashing of goose grease on your chest and back? It was fatty, evil smelling and rubbed into the skin, which glistened under the friction. It was reckoned to be a cure for all ailments, ranging from pneumonia, consumption, aching backs, rheumatism, pessimism and even Communism.

Goose grease was almost as potent, pungent, and downright smelly as a Kaolin poultice, which was applied red hot to affected parts and covered with flannel. How or why these remedies often worked wonders is beyond me. It does not seem possible or practical that the properties contained in such basic substances could pierce skin and layers of fat to relieve pain and result in total cure of various maladies. They were termed 'old wife's remedies' and cynics scoffed at them.

Such treatments worked in many cases and, although I prefer mustard on ham sandwiches, I remember my extremely sore feet felt much better after dangling them for half an hour in a bath laced with salt and mustard powder. I also recall sharing a bedroom with my younger brother Ted, and it wasn't much fun when he had one of his regular 'attacks'. I preferred the haunting aroma of oxtail to the peculiar odour of Kaolin, sulphur candles, Do-Do tablets, Yeastvite and the other concoctions which were poured into my asthmatic sibling. We never tried Roboleine on him as far as I know, and he probably missed out on something extra special.

However, I am now sucking a Zube and filling my glass with a good measure of Parrish's Food to drink to your good health. Or has the Lovely Maureen given me the wrong bottle which contains something labelled the Famous Grouse?

Sweet Memories

'Where would you buy ice-cream in the desert?' asked Jimmy, a schoolboy of eight tender years and a laddie destined to be the life and soul of any party when he reaches manhood.

'Would it be Walls of Jericho?' I ventured.

'No, Lyons of Judah', replied the budding Ken Dodd.

I sympathised with an ice-cream vendor recently. The weather was bitterly cold. He shivered behind frosted van windows. And ding-dong chimes announced that he had arrived in the futile hope of selling some of his frozen assets. He had no chance. Kiddies resisted the invitation. Even the offer of free tutti-fruttis would have been rejected by ice-cream addicts who shivered and opted for the comforting warmth of the fireside.

It doesn't take me long to plunge into a bout of memories. I often ask myself 'Is nostalgia a thing of the past?', but I make no apology for wallowing in a reverie of idle recapitulation.

Do you remember the 'Wallsy' man? He used to wear a white and black peaked cap, white jacket, and white and blue striped trousers. He pedalled a bike which had a square blue freezer in front. He rang a bell and his message was 'Stop me and buy one'. We used to laugh and holler: 'Knock him down and pinch one'. Not that we ever seriously considered such an anti-social and illegal action. A man could propel his 'ice-cycle' without fear of assault or robbery in those days.

The man from Walls sold 'Snofrutes'. They were fore-runners of the ice-lollies kiddies ruin their teeth on today. But they were so different in taste. They were encased in a triangular cardboard tube. They dripped as you sucked. And the melting juice often ran over your hand between your fingers and down your arm. I can feel its sticky warmth just thinking about it. Your teeth would go on edge if they touched the cardboard. It was like sampling Fennings fever cure.

But we relished choc-ices, milk and plain ones, and our spending money often went in one mad spree on a tub of ice-cream. It was topped with a splash of sweet vinegar, the colour of Wincarnis tonic wine, and eaten with a flat wooden spoon.

Pocket money of tuppence and threepence went a long way, and a Saturday run to the sweet shop, before the afternoon film matinee, was a treat and a must.

Do you remember biting into hard sticks of black spanish which almost pulled the molars from the back of your head? Do you remember brown spanish bootlaces and the spanish wound tightly round a pink or white sweet? I am sure you do. And you will probably recall aniseed balls — they made you spit blood; gob-stoppers, which changed colour the more you sucked; Virginia, which resembled strands of brown tobacco; and liquorice, a chewy root with a taste which made you grimace and cleaned your teeth at the same time.

Do your saliva buds start to moisten when you recall the lip-smacking ecstasy of kali? You could buy it in a three-cornered packet, or in a yellow paper-wrapped tube with a spanish sucker sticking out to draw the lemon-flavoured powder into your mouth. If you didn't fancy that, you wet your fingers, dabbed them in the powder, and almost sucked the skin off the discoloured digits as you basked in the delights of this delectable concoction.

Cinder toffee had that burnt taste. Lucky bags were a magical treat and a venture into the realm of expectancy. You never knew what goodies would be lurking among the handful of dolly mixtures, sherbets and midget all-sorts. By gum and by jelly babies they were good.

I'm glad I bumped into Jimmy and listened to his riddles.

The Golden Days of Silverdale

My first 'holiday' was a day trip on a vehicle with solid rubber tyres ambitiously described as a charabanc, and the tiny passengers felt every bump as it occasionally backfired from Castleford to the green slopes of Ledston Luck.

The outing was a gift to children of the neighbourhood by the local bookmaker Sam Boldison, who also provided the bangers, parkin, treacle toffee and sparklers at the annual Guy Fawkes bonfire. Relatives and friends waved goodbye to toddlers who clutched a lucky bag containing sweets, sandwich and an apple. But even these could not stem the tears from kiddies who believed that Ledston Luck was a million miles away and they were leaving home for good. I didn't cry. I was a 'big boy' and often spent weekends in Leeds with my mother's family and regarded myself as a seasoned traveller, having commuted from Marsh Lane Railway Station, Leeds, to Castleford. But a 'holiday', if only for a day, was a rare treat and remains a memory which — though fleeting in detail — has stayed with me close on sixty-five years.

It was years later before Blackpool became our annual holiday, and I remember the long, tiring queues for coaches and trains during the war years. We clutched our luggage, including gas-masks in cardboard boxes, and prayed we would arrive safely at the double delights of beach and briny.

I was a reporter working at Cartmel racecourse before I had the chance to visit Morecambe, the Lancashire resort loved by comedian Albert Modley and the butt of the late Colin Crompton's acid wit.

But I was back at Morecambe recently via Silverdale, and a special and memorable visit to the Leeds Children's Holiday Camp. My mother Norah worked in the Silverdale laundry before the First World War, and often told me as a child that we were not 'poor' enough to spend a holiday there. She also told me that she couldn't afford to give me two Christian names at my baptism, and I believed both tales for years.

Silverdale was known as the Leeds Poor Children's Holiday Camp, but 'Poor' — an unintentional slur on the financial plights of families — was deleted after a campaign launched by several Leeds citizens, including Bert and Fred of the celebrated Gaunt Brothers. The camp was founded in 1904 by a group of generous Leeds people concerned for the city's needy children. They met to consider how best to bring sunshine and fresh air into young lives, and eight acres of picturesque scenery overlooking Morecambe Bay were secured. The history of the beautiful location does not always reflect 'sweetness and light'. But the fact remains that many youngsters would otherwise not have seen the sea, enjoyed regular meals and escaped the grime of slums for a fortnight.

Our group was greeted by thirty-six bright-eyed children from varying backgrounds. It was a cheerful welcome, with songs galore, and a conducted tour round the trim and homely premises. Toni was my guide. Her description of the holiday was complimentary, even though she admitted to a tinge of homesickness. If there was one impish observation, it came from a pink-cheeked lassie who told me: 'It isn't as good as Majorca where I went with my nan.'

'In 1941 I spent two wonderful happy weeks at this splendid place', Barbara Garety of Leeds told me. 'Many years later I took my young children, driving all the way from Wimbledon. They were not impressed. The magic suddenly changed from those far-off sunny days when simple pleasures were far better than what is on offer today. But in my heart it will always be the happiest two weeks of my young life.'

Dixieland and All That Jazz

Leeds Town Hall is an imposing structure, and the exterior — though cleaner than it used to be — has not undergone many, if any, significant changes. However, the interior has altered greatly since the days when the British Restaurant provided wartime fare for city-centre workers. Fried fish and chips — if you were early enough — was the pick of the menu, and infinitely superior to Lord Woolton pie with mash, or spam fritters.

But the place blessed with outstanding grandeur is still the majestic Victoria Hall, the scene of so many memorable activities — concerts, dances, organ recitals, orchestral and choral productions, and, for those with a sporting appetite, wrestling and boxing.

I remember dancing with the Lovely Maureen to Johnny Adlestone's band when Adrian Hill, who became Ronnie Hilton, was the regular vocalist. Those Friday night 'hops' were the highlight of our courting days, although we patronised other projects like lunchtime piano recitals. Anyone prepared to skip lunch from 12.30 to 1.30 could enjoy these free performances of classical music.

My appetite for such uplifting musical experiences was not exactly voracious. I confess I was something of a classical music Philistine, but I reluctantly attended to impress the more discerning Maureen, and she in turn agreed to accompany me and endure the wonderful nights of Dixieland jazz which transported us from Leeds Town Hall to Chicago, New Orleans and Harlem every Sunday night.

Those concerts came to mind when I learned that Nat Gonella — trumpeter and band leader — had celebrated his ninety-second birthday. The first record I bought from Kitchens in Leeds featured Joe Daniel and his Hotshots, and I was hooked on swinging jazz from that day. The second was by the eternal Gonella, and years later I interviewed him at the City Varieties, where, in between bursts on his trumpet, he answered my questions. Before he went on stage I asked him if he would play *Sentimental Interlude*, and he shook his head, apologised and said: 'I'm sorry but it is not in our programme.'

Ten minutes into his act with his band the New Georgians, Nat announced:

'There is a young man in the circle who has specially requested a very old number. I only hope I can remember it.'

Nat certainly did recall the haunting refrain. His gravelled voice sang every word, pausing only to produce the inimitable Gonella sound from his trumpet.

Nat's signature tune *Georgia On My Mind* was a hit record even with those with only the remotest interest in jazz.

Jazz at Leeds Town Hall had a huge and loyal following. We enjoyed the regular concerts before the advent of skiffle, which was followed by the guitar-twanging pop groups of the sixties and the outbreak of new-wave music from such bands as the Beatles and Rolling Stones. Of course they will be remembered in years to come, just as some of us recall the golden age of the jazz-band scene in Yorkshire. Do you remember tapping your feet to Freddie Randle, the Tomassos, Harry Gold and his Pieces Of Eight, Ken Colyer, Humphrey Lyttleton and his mate Wally Fawkes, Alex Welsh, George Melly and a Manchester band called the Saints? And what about Eddie O'Donnell, who is still going strong?

Loving thy Neighbour

Mrs Mullen cut a frail figure under the blue-and-white striped apron she wore in the style of a market butcher. She was an excellent cook. But her family of growing lads had the lion's share and major portions. She learned how to tighten the belt of her pinafore and do without. I remember her saying:

'I had a walk round the table for dinner. And another one for my tea. It was enough for me.'

Mrs Mullen pecked at left-overs. She was just one of the many thin and self-sacrificing ladies we had as neighbours in days of prewar unemployment, long dole queues and depressing austerity.

She was tiny. But, strange to relate, she had ponderous arms. The tops bulged like Popeye's biceps. There was a dimple at her elbows, from which billowed forearms of Henry Cooper proportions. The limbs, which were always outstretched to circle infants in a loving cuddle, drew their strength and size from pounding laundry, wringing out washing with hands and wrists, and kneading a dollop of dough three times a week to bake the staff of life for her ever-increasing and always-hungry offspring.

Mrs Mullen sang Gracie Fields numbers with the sweet nightingale quality of the lass from Rochdale as she pummelled the flour, yeast, fat, milk and water into a consistency ready for dropping into greased loaf-tins. She guessed the amount and weight of ingredients. She was always right. And her arms worked like pistons, with fists punching the animated mountain of floured mixture. She baked without recourse to Mrs Beeton's cookery book or any other culinary guide, and she knew to the second when the risen dough was ready for the oven. Her bread was rich and crumbly, delicious when warm, with melting butter running through the holes like honey in a comb.

When she mixed dough, she always gave a tiny portion to children entranced by her enthusiastic labours. We patted it between our palms, rolled it like plasticine. And as our grubby little hands turned pink and clean, the dough took on a decidedly grey hue. Of course it went into the oven. But the hard-as-iron end-product was for showing to an admiring audience and certainly not for consumption.

Mrs Mullen was one of countless families of Irish extraction that settled at a place renowned within the Leeds boundaries as the Bank. It was an area brimming with colourful characters and overflowing with neighbourly love. Inhabitants were simple people. They worked and worshipped and collected pennies to build Mount St Mary's Church, which towered above the dwellings. The grimy bricked houses had eerie cellars, setpots and staircases built for mountain goats.

The Bank had a famous policeman called Rocking Horse. He was a small constable with bent legs. It gave him a rocking gait when he broke into a chase of one minor miscreant or another. And he preferred to give the law-breakers a smart clip across the ear as opposed to dragging them off to the cop shop. Legend has it that he never made an arrest because he did not know how to fill out a charge sheet. He opted for instant justice, and he would rather crack a few heads than have the fuss and bother of locking a lad in the local nick.

The names PC Gilford and PC Sapcoat will be remembered by many, who also recall with equal clarity Mrs Power. She ran a sweet shop, and smashed slabs of brittle toffee into chewable pieces with a tiny metal hammer. When the toffee containers were empty, she gave them away to mums who used them as oven trays.

They were hard but happy days. Families depended on each other. Neighbours helped to peg out the washing. If the lady of the house was 'confined', she could rely on the folk next door to make her home ship-shape for the arrival of the doctor and midwife for the everyday occurrence — another home delivery of another new baby. People were kind and considerate. They shared each other's joys, blessings and tragedies. They celebrated births and they mourned at the wakes — those mysterious nocturnal gatherings where prayers were chanted and vigils kept before the remains of a loved one were taken to the local church for a service prior to burial.

It was at such a wake where an immortal invitation was extended to all who came to keep watch and express sympathy to the bereaved. The man in charge of the inevitable bottles of sherry, gin and whisky, and a drop of the home-made hard stuff, sidled to the visitors. With due solemnity he asked.

'The corpse's brother wants to know if you will take a drink with us.'

The answer to the corpse's brother's request was always in the affirmative.

There was another wake when a lady placed her empty tea cup and saucer on the coffin of the dearly departed. She realised in an instant what she had done. She picked up the crockery, rubbed away the wet ring it had left on the woodwork, and she gazed at the chap reposing in his shroud.

'Oops, sorry Fred', she murmured. 'I didn't realise you were in there. You'll be the death of me.'

The lady was Mrs Mullen, who went to her eternal resting place a decade or two ago. But memories of the kindly soul invariably conjure visions of the Bank, with its poverty and also its fun-loving community. I talked to one of Mrs Mullen's white-haired 'youngsters' last week. We agreed that his grandmother was a tiny lass, but a giant when it came to baking lovely bread.

The Great Theatres we Lost

There was a time when the future of the West Yorkshire Playhouse in Leeds was as dark as a badly illuminated auditorium. But a campaign to rescue the financially troubled centre of elegance and culture succeeded in protecting this theatrical treasure for posterity.

It is a pity that similar salvage action was not launched to maintain the existence of the Leeds Theatre Royal, Leeds Empire and hundreds of similar edifices of entertainment. The Theatre Royal closed its portals on the 1st April 1957, and it was a significant date because it was a foolish decision to rob the city of a beloved landmark. The final performance was watched by a capacity audience of 1,600, and at the end of the show *Queen of Hearts* the curtain descended slowly to the beat of a muted drum roll. It was an evening charged with emotion, and a farewell address written by Mrs Gwladys Laidler was read by Wilfred Pickles. Comedian Eddie Henderson made a brave but feeble attempt to lift the gloom.

'Don't be sad', he quipped. 'They have pulled down every place I've worked in.'

The following day 1,600 seats were removed, and many were bought by amateur theatrical companies. Fittings and fixtures followed, and eventually bulldozers moved in to clear a site for new owners Schofields — now replaced and renamed the Schofields Centre.

The Leeds Empire opened on the 29th August 1898, with a seating capacity of 2,000, and the first managing director was Edward Moss, later knighted for services to the theatrical world. Edward suffered from first-night nerves, and started with an unintentional Spoonerism which had the audience in hysterics: 'Ladies and gentlemen, I won't occutime your pie.'

The patrons were described by top-of-the-bill comedian Harry Tate as 'magnificent and distinguished'. They 'greatly approved' of the ornate structure and gasped with amazement at the latest innovation, a sliding roof which opened to allow smoke out, the moon to be seen and the odd dicky bird to enter.

The Empire ceased to function on the 25th February 1961, with Six Royal Welshmen singing 'God Save The Queen' and the cast of *Babes in the Wood* joining in. Among those saying goodbye to the 'Lost Empire' were manager Leo Lion, a dapper executive; musical director Ronnie Roberts, who was also landlord at the Woodman Inn, Selby Road; barmaid Helen Wheatley, who was Nellie to thousands of Empire regulars; and probably the best-known employee, Charles McConomy. Leo started life in the theatre as a call-boy and shared these duties with Val Parnell, a chap destined to become a national impresario.

Nellie worked in the dress circle bar for forty-five years, when Bass was fourpence a bottle, whisky fourpence a tot and liqueurs sixpence. Charles McConomy was Charlie to regulars, and he wore a blue uniform with the job description 'Foreman' picked out in gold letters. He was a master of all theatre trades, but he loved to mingle with the Briggate crowds shouting 'Seats in all parts'.

Charlie was the last to leave the Empire. He stayed to help clear the demolished area. He was not too dispirited because — like many of us — he truly believed that another music hall would rise from the debris. But now only memories remain of the era when laughter and applause echoed in those icons of varied entertainment.

The Art of Sparing One's Blushes

Was my face red! How many times have you uttered those words after pitching headlong — often unwittingly — into one embarrassing predicament or another to emerge with the glow of a crimson flush creeping from the nape of your neck to the roots of your crowning glory? The majority of people want the ground to open when faults and shortcomings are exposed to the world at large.

But there are those who can brazen out any situation. Such a man was the reporter Dave Thompson, who made regular and headlong sorties into the most ticklish situations but always emerged smelling of the proverbial roses. He was once detailed to attend a lavish function with his wife. And the welcome presence of a free bar was like manna to a scribbler who cheerfully admitted that he worked better with his larynx suitably lubricated. Dave almost wore a track in the carpet as he marched up to the bar for constant refills. His gait became unsteadier as the evening progressed, and eventually his long-suffering spouse decided to shame him into some semblance of sobriety. Mrs Thompson made sure everyone in the room heard her objection as she hollered:

'Dave, that must be the tenth time you have been to the bar for a large whisky. Doesn't it embarrass you?'

This was a signal for a hush to descend on the gathering. Every eye was trained on Dave, who simply raised his drink to his lips and replied:

'Why should I be embarrassed, my love? I keep telling the barman the drinks are for you.'

Another 'sensitive' scribe was the late Con Gordon, who furthered my journalistic education when I was a mere stripling. He taught me that no matter how pretty a pickle I might mix for myself, no jam, scrape, fix or quandary is insoluble or insurmountable. He was an object lesson in diplomacy, and I recall with affection and a modicum of envy his discreet exit from a spot of bother during a wartime assignment.

Rationing was in full force. There was a shortage of everything, and particularly fresh meat. In fact the first time I saw a butcher's shop festooned with hanging meat I thought there had been an accident. Worried mums queued with ration books for the weekly allowance of a couple of bobsworth of stewing steak, and the dearth of good old roast beef was beginning to embarrass even the government. But rescue was at hand. There was a sudden glut of herrings on the market. And the Minister of Food, Lord Woolton, decided that a dash of propaganda was essential to encourage the populace to switch their yearning appetites and taste buds from four-legged creatures to those with fins. And so gentlemen of the press — including Con Gordon and I — were invited to listen to an expert extolling the virtues of the 'four-eyed steak'.

A couple of dozen reporters arrived at the ministry offices, but Con was late and the talk began without his commanding presence. Just inside the entrance was a colossal display of herrings. They were soused, pickled, fried, boiled, grilled and cooked in a multitude of different ways. The press representatives were duly impressed. We were summoned into another room, where our Man from the Ministry delivered his talk and then announced:

'Gentlemen, we will now move into the exhibition area, where an eminent chef from a leading hotel will explain in detail the number of different ways one can prepare the humble herring for the gastronomic delight of all members of the family.'

We retraced our steps to the entrance, and there we discovered Con finishing off the last of the herrings. He smacked his lips, licked his fingers, and left a pile of bones and fish-heads reminiscent of a scene from the *Dandy* after Korky The Cat had finished off a posh nosh at the Hotel Splendide. There was a howl of protest from the minister's representative. There was a squeal of anguish from the frustrated cook. There was a hiss of disapproval from reporters who had been robbed of a fish-tasting session. And there wasn't a hint of remorse or embarrassment from the errant but now replete diner.

'The herrings ...', gasped the spokesman.

'Were very nice, acceptable, but probably could have done with an extra dash of vinegar', interspersed Con as he turned on his heel and stalked from the wreckage with as much swagger as he could muster. I was lost in admiration.

There was another time when our reporter, the late Ken Lemmon, charged into a gas board meeting, where a colossal buffet awaited the hungry horde of news hounds. Ken picked up a family-sized pork pie. He took a mouthful and stared into the disapproving face of a chap who announced:

'I will be speaking for the next half hour and then declare the buffet open.'

Ken didn't blush. He simply lowered the pie behind his back, where he cradled and nursed it for the thirty minutes. And the official droned on to prove that he could produce as much hot air as the company he represented.

Many Yorkshiremen have a degree of sensitivity. Panic rages at the mere mention of a crisis, as it did a couple of years ago when I entered a store to buy a suit.

'Short and portly this way', the lady shopwalker smiled benevolently. I would have died a dozen deaths had she started to measure me.

Yorkshiremen are supposed to have a strong personality, bordering on domineering. We are termed bluff and jovial. But I blushed recently. Boy how I blushed. First of all, a student offered me his seat on a bus. And to rub salt into the gaping wound, the local barber stood at his till and volunteered: 'Pensioners half-price this week, John.'

Was my face red!

Waves of Fear

You probably remember sailing on the *Yorkshireman* or the *Boys Own* from Bridlington Harbour and enjoying a panoramic view of the coast. But I went one better when the jolly crew of the local lifeboat invited TV steeplejack Fred Dibnah and me to join them on a Saturday morning exercise.

Unlike me, Fred wasn't bothered. He is a small, chunky man of uncertain age. He is rarely seen without his flat cap. He makes after-dinner speeches with it pulled down tightly on his thinning hair, when he talks about scaling three hundred feet chimneys as though he was embarking on a Sunday morning stroll.

'Tha'll be reight. Tha's nowt to worry about,' said the Bolton-based Lancastrian who — I can exclusively reveal — hails from Yorkshire stock.

'My mam and dad were from Hull. But I like to keep that a secret. Don't tell more than a hundred', added Fred who, apart from blowing up chimney stacks and supping pints, has a passion for collecting steam engines and rebuilding the 'ruddy monsters'.

Fred and me arrived at the lifeboat station with one of us facing the imminent ordeal with trepidation and a churning stomach. The thought struck me that the last will and testament I made was completed when I did my National Service. I wondered if it was still valid, and I also mentally checked if my life insurance premiums were up-to-date.

It was a wonderful experience, with coxswain Fred Walkington describing the sea as 'placid', even though the billowing swell looked to my untrained eye as though it would erupt into gigantic waves of storm proportions. But quaking thoughts of another *Titanic* disaster quickly evaporated. We even discovered a boat showing signs of distress with a 'dicky' engine, and although we escorted him back to safety we could not exactly describe it as an official rescue. Fred and me took turns at steering our craft, and the views of the magnificent coastal scenery made me forget the lining of breakfast egg and bacon I felt would surely surface as the voyage proceeded. I was sorry when the trip came to an end, and it was only when the lifeboat was hauled from the beach and back to base the thought struck me that I was the only member of the crew not equipped with a life jacket. It must have been an oversight. The jolly jaunt ended in style with a steam engine — made by the Hunslet Engineering Company in 1920 — standing in all its smoking glory on the promenade to welcome Fred.

Bridlington was one of two favourite resorts for the Lovely Maureen and me when our offspring were at the bucket and spade age. The other one was Filey, and I still wince at the thoughts of pushing our Silver Cross pram up the steep climb from the golden sands.

We often failed to resist the lure of a boat trip when sailors shouted:

'Twice around the Bay and back in time for tea.'

We went on the *Yorkshireman* and *Boys Own*, and sampled the delights of the saloon bar before joining in the sing-along with the accordion player. We also sailed on the *Coronia* at Scarborough and the *Regal Lad*. And I think there was also a *Yorkshire Lady* and a *Regency Belle*. No doubt you will tell me if I am wrong.

Love for Lizzie

Woodbine Lizzie died in Stanley Royd Hospital, Wakefield, in 1947. But she is remembered by thousands of Leeds folk who either exchanged the time of day or skirted round the unkempt lady. She spent the greater part of her life as a tramp. She puffed 'woodies' as she traipsed through the city centre. But her regular haunt was the passage leading to the Whip public house on Duncan Street, Leeds. Woodbine Lizzie stood there for hours, usually dressed in several coats, with a basket over one arm, a bag and raincoat over the other, and a tram conductor's hat perched on her straggly hair.

My first close contact with Lizzie came in the Liptons store in Kirkgate when I joined an orderly queue of women clutching ration books. Suddenly there was a mad scramble

for the exit. The shoppers hurried from the premises, clearing a passage for me ... and Lizzie. It was only when I saw horror on the face of the man turning the handle of the bacon slicer that I became aware of Lizzie's presence. She fingered a few biscuits in an open tin and the assistant barked: 'Take 'em and clear off.'

Lizzie put them in one of her bags, grinned and left with her mission accomplished.

Lizzie was feted during the war by the Eighth Army in the Middle East. The transporters usually carried the names of ladies, and in one desert compound the BBC reporter Godfrey Talbot spotted 'Kathleen from Bradford, Gwen of Llandudno and Woodbine Lizzie from Leeds'. Godfrey broadcast the story, and when Lizzie was acquainted of the honour she growled: 'My name should be on a tank'.

Many remember Woodbine Lizzie with obvious affection. Others ran a mile when she came into view, and there is no doubt that she had an earthy turn of phrase — especially when children jeered. Several folk advance the claim that she was born in a good family and was disappointed in love. Others repeat the theory that she was the illegitimate daughter of a nobleman who disowned her at birth.

In fact her true identity was Mrs Alice Porter, wife and mother, and she reverted to this name when her marriage ended. She was born in Stanningley, and at eighteen she moved with her parents to Pudsey. In the same year she married Joe Hartley. They produced six children in twelve years, including five boys.

'The marriage was over during the First World War', Lizzie said. 'We simply did not hit it off. I was thirty-eight when I abandoned my home and became a vagabond — a lady tramp to you.'

Lizzie claimed that the open air helped her to survive because she was a 'weakling' from the day she was born and weighed under nine stone during her pregnancies. She said:

'I was always able to look after myself and I had more guts than most folk. I've never been unhappy, although I was sad when I had to leave the kids. I love to sing and have a good voice, even though I say so myself.'

But that opinion was not shared by those who teased her about the lifestyle she had chosen — or her appearance. Her language could strip paint at a hundred yards. She was hoarse and strident — a legacy from life in the open, chest problems and her passion for Woodbines.

Woodbine Lizzie would have been my first interview as a reporter had she not 'fightened' this wary teenager to death. We seem to lack such harmless but colourful characters these days — more's the pity.

TTFN ... I'm off to Listen to my Radio

Do you find yourself mesmerised by television and abruptly emerge from a trance to discover that the most banal and trivial drivel is beaming from the screen? I am convinced that the 'box' exerts hypnotic domination and has an irresistible control on our frail willpower.

My cheeks glow with crimson embarrassment at the mere mention of *Neighbours* — the puerile Australian 'soap' which is an insult to even infantile intelligence. Haven't our antipodean cousins inflicted sufficient punishment on us in the sporting sphere without rubbing the salt of *Neighbours* into our gaping wounds? However, confession is good for the soul and, to my eternal shame, I admit that the recent adventures of totally unbelievable Harold, Madge, Lou, Toadfish and others have been followed by this once-discerning television viewer. I must have taken leave of the few senses left in my creaking cerebellum to have even contemplated watching it.

But never again. From now on it is the old reliable wireless for me — a medium which informs and entertains without the necessity of focussing weary old eyes on the flickering images. There was a time when the radio was regarded as miraculous and a prime example of the wonders the modern world had in store. And the thought of men landing on the moon, and the computerised transmission of words and pictures, were simply in the vivid imagination of *Flash Gordon* scriptwriters and scribblers of *Dan Dare* stories.

One of the pioneers of steam radio was Tommy Handley, who was destined to revolutionise comedy, lighten the war years, lift and maintain morale, and introduce catchphrases which are still in common use. Many of us recall those days of austerity and anxiety when rationing and the ever-present threat to loved ones in the services plunged the nation into a mood as dark and forbidding as the nightly blackout. The family radio was an essential boost to flagging spirits, with inspiring words from Winston Churchill, news broadcasts by Alvar Liddell, and entertaining moments with *Workers' Playtime*, *Children's Hour*, *Music While You Work*, *Monday Night At Eight*, *In Town Tonight* and Tommy Handley's show *ITMA*.

It was quickfire comic Tommy who reduced the programme name of *It's That Man Again* to the bare initials *ITMA*. He finished the broadcast with TTFN — 'ta ta for now' — and, in between, squeezed interruptions from Mrs Mopp — 'Can I do you now sir?'; Mona Lott, telling us 'It's being so cheerful that keeps me going'; the effete pals with 'After you, Claude', 'No after you, Cecil'; and Colonel Chinstrap adding 'I don't mind if I do'. There were so many lines which became part of everyday speech and, at its peak, *ITMA* had a listening audience of sixteen million fans, including the Royal family. *ITMA* was broadcast from 1939 to 1949, but on the 9th January of that year Tommy died, and the country mourned his passing with thousands thronging pavements as his cortège wended a sad journey to the comedian's resting place.

ITMA set a pattern for romantic lads and lasses who posted letters with SWALK — 'sealed with a loving kiss' — on the back of the envelope. HOLLAND — 'hope our love lasts and never dies' — was another, and others used BOLTOP with a line of kisses. It meant 'better on lips than on paper'. Shyness prevents me from explaining the meaning of BURMA, and no doubt you will tell each other. But for the moment it is TTFN from me and GFE for *Neighbours*. That means Goodbye For Eternity.

Albert and the Jet Set

Albert and his missus Mary Ellen are creatures of habit. They have been to Filey every year since they were wed and wouldn't dream of holidaying elsewhere. They are members at the local British Legion club, where Albert knocks back a few pints, plays a nifty game of billiards and turns in a useful display of crown green bowling when summer arrives. They subscribe to the maxim 'We like to pay our corner', and they often 'thoil' the occasional club outing, providing the 'chara' takes them somewhere in their beloved Filey region.

So you can imagine the upheaval, hubbub and tingling excitement when their eldest son sent them airfares from Yorkshire to Canada with the request that his dear old parents should pay him and his family a flying visit. Blood pressure was in danger of soaring to fever pitch as the day of departure drew near. Mary Ellen allowed herself a visit to Marks and Sparks as opposed to a search of the nearly-new merchandise at the local Oxfam and Mind establishments.

'You ought to get yourself one of those lumber jackets. All Canadians wear them', she advised Albert. But her advice fell on stony ground.

When she and Albert finally boarded the plane, he sported the usual blue serge suit, waistcoat, matching socks and well-polished shoes. Albert reasoned that if the outfit was good enough for the annual Remembrance Parade, it was good enough for cutting Canadian capers.

Neither had flown before. They would have done, had there been pleasure flights to Filey. But before halfway, Albert and Mary Ellen were seasoned travellers. He thanked the hostess profusely for her service and even tried to settle up for his free drinks. Albert and Mary Ellen always paid their corner.

'Boing boing', went the tannoy and the hostess announced: 'In approximately six minutes we will be landing at Vancouver. We do hope you have enjoyed your flight.'

Albert leapt to his feet. He had been on enough tours and club trips to know that one important task had been overlooked. Albert pulled off his cap and started his 'whip-round for the driver'. Albert's cap bulged. The cash almost burst his headgear from the neb to the press-stud. And he proudly handed it to the hostess to give to the 'driver'.

'Boing boing', went the tannoy, followed by: 'This is your captain speaking. Gee folks, I have been flying these crates for twenty-five years and this is the first time there has been a collection for me and the crew. We are very grateful. May I say a big thank you for the money — over £500 — and we will drink your health tonight.'

Albert settled back in his seat. He fastened his safety belt. He smiled at Mary Ellen. She squeezed his hand. Others might have forgotten, but her Albert hadn't. They had paid their corner again.

The Toast of the Taws

My pal Eric did not know the meaning of the word fear. In fact he didn't know the meaning of most words, but he was a dab hand at taws.

Eric was a lad of advanced physique, and he grew in strength if not in wisdom. Eric had a suspect temperament. It was prudent to steer clear of him when his dander was up. And it would certainly have soared had he shared an experience with me the other day.

My thoughts flashed to Eric's skill at taws, when I picked up a box of them in a local store. There was a potted history of marbles inside, and Eric's dander would have exploded had he read this missive on the art of knuckling glass 'alleys'. My wrath reached fever pitch because the author of the booklet dismissed us with the terse mention: 'Marbles were sometimes played in the North'. I can feel the blood rising again. Surely the ancient pastime was invented by Yorkshiremen, and if it wasn't, it should have been.

My introduction to taws goes back to infant life in Castleford. It was renowned in those days for rugby legends Juicy Adams and Bruss Atkinson, leading citizens Ezra Taylor and Gideon Shaw, bookie Sam Boldison, cricketer Frank Ambler and Bannisters fish and chip shop. One of our neighbours was burgeoning sculptor Henry Moore — probably a taws man — but the town was really put on the marbles map when Lady Docker, with hubby Bernard in tow, deserted their ocean-going yacht for a visit to Cas and participation in the world taws championships. Lady Docker had many attributes, but she was useless at flipping glass 'alleys'.

My pal Eric wasn't. He aimed taws with the speed and accuracy of an Exocet missile. He was unbeatable at our game, which was so different to the one outlined in the marbles booklet. Our pitch was any patch of waste ground. One player would revolve on his heel to make a hole known as a 'knack'. This was just as important as the ledge from which the game started. The ledge was a causey edge or maybe just a line scraped a few feet from the knack.

Taws were as popular with Yorkshire lads as beddy, tig and kick-out can. Colourful glass 'alleys' were prized possessions, and so were 'stonkers', made, as the name suggests, from stone.

The game started with one player 'plugging' his taw on the pitch. His rival would fire from the ledge, and experts like Eric gripped the taw between thumb and finger to propel the aerial onslaught from raised knee-cap. If he hit the target, he then aimed for the knack, and if his taw dropped in a hole he collected his rival's 'alley'. But there were tricks to render the simple exercise difficult. You have to be as quick with the tongue as the taw. If you shouted 'No rounds, tibs, bonks, bobs or over', the opposing player could not hit your taw and had to play a safety shot. You were sometimes accused of 'sticking your neb', which meant you advanced the knuckle beyond the accepted point of delivery.

One did not take such a liberty with lads like Eric. You simply endured hours of blissful play, and went home with sore knuckles, mucky knees and the pockets of your short pants bulging with taws or painfully empty of the beautiful baubles.

That Flagging Feeling

'Buy a flag, please', implored the teenager, sticking his tin under my chin. 'It's a good cause.'

'Aren't they all?' I growled. And the miserly reaction earned from the Lovely Maureen a stinging rebuke suggesting that I would give Scrooge a run for his money.

'Don't make a song and dance about it. Give with a charitable heart or not at all', she said.

I suppose she is right. She usually is. But there is a persistent call on your pockets these days, with lads and lasses getting up to all manner of sponsored activities, various collections, benefits and testimonials, not to mention the interminable list of engagement and wedding presents for colleagues you never knew existed until a complete stranger approaches with news of the impending nuptials.

We often claim that so-and-so has short arms and deep pockets. We allege that he could peel an orange in his pocket or that the same is filled with fish-hooks. But one of my pals practises the thrifty streak for sheer fun. He loves to act the part of a meany, even though he secretly gives to many charitable causes. He claims that he was married in the back yard so the hens could eat the rice. And I remember him surprising us all by suddenly announcing that he intended to throw a party. One of the astonished guests was given the following instructions on how to get in to his flat:

'Come up to the fifth floor and ring the doorbell with your elbow. When the door opens, push with your foot.'

'Why my elbow and foot?', the puzzled chap queried.

The 'miser' replied: 'You won't be coming empty-handed will you?'

There was another time when he owed quite a sum of money. His creditor called, listened to the tale of financial woe, and made a magnanimious gesture.

'I am prepared to show you how generous I can be', the benefactor said. 'I will forget half the debt.'

'And I'll prove to you how generous I can be', my relieved and grateful mate answered. 'I'll forget the other half.'

He squared his account eventually, and he is as charitable as the next man. But he will never be as cute as the

shopkeeper who placed a tin on his counter and labelled it 'For The Blind'. People popped coins and notes into the cannister, which disappeared within a week. And shoppers noticed a new blind rolling up and down inside the window.

A few weeks ago a young man called round to Morgan Manor and announced: 'I'm rowing a boat to raise money for St Gemma's Hospice. Will you sponsor me?'

It was probably not an opportune moment to call. It was a busy day. I had probably emerged from the bed on the wrong side. 'I do enough for St Gemma's', I barked.

I wanted the ground to swallow me when the lad murmured: 'My dad died there'.

Naturally my attitude changed. Sometimes you need a jolt. And by golly I deserved mine. You should give until it hurts and — as the Lovely Maureen claims — 'with a good heart'. And I don't mean only money. A priest once explained charity to me. He said:

'It is: Silence — when your words would hurt. Patience — when your neighbour is curt. Deafness — when a scandal flows. Thoughtfulness — for others' woes. Prompted — when duty calls. Courage — when misfortune falls.'

All that — and a few bob too when you can spare it.

On the Tracks of Memory

A small, oblong framed picture on the wall in the hotel bedroom looked vaguely familiar. But it was the caption which really jogged my memory. It simply read: 'A view of Peebles'. And I knew from where it came.

Do you recall the prints of spots like Grange Over Sands or Burnham-on-Sea in the old-style railway carriages in the age of steam? Train compartments had straight-up seats with arm rests you could pull down. There was a sort of string hammock overhead for luggage, and underneath were pictures of places like Peebles. Carriages usually lacked the basic requirement of a corridor and a loo.

Trips to and from Blackpool often took three to four hours, and I recall a wartime journey when it was even longer. We were shunted into sidings to allow a troop train to pass, much to the dismay and distress of a male passenger who had spent an hour in a seaside pub, and whose condition was becoming desperate. We youngsters were all agog when a

considerate young lady — realising his predicament — pointed to our buckets and spades, and suggested that we could all turn our backs. The gentleman smiled his gratitude but he refused. When we halted at Skipton, two hefty youths had to carry him across the platform to the gents.

Growing Pains

Edward Jones was a genius. There is no doubt about that. He was a man of multi-talents, a one-off, and the inscription on his tombstone listed only a few of his gifted attributes. It read:

'Edward Jones. Poet, Inventor, Vagabond, Musician, Dreamer, Philosopher and Landscape Gardener.'

The adjoining grave had a similar headstone with the words: 'Edna Jones — long-suffering wife of Edward Jones.'

Edward was a daydreamer. He squandered fortunes on the hair-brained schemes he produced in fevered bouts of contemplation. But he also made pots of money from gardening. He was not only a son of the soil, but a creative artist when faced with the challenge of turning a wilderness into a display of incredible beauty. He used to advertise in the local paper:

'Don't kill yourself in the garden. Let me do it for you.'

I thought of Edward yesterday when I saw an elderly chap taking a breather from a back-breaking bout of tilling Mother Earth. I have never been a keen gardener. And I used to annoy the Lovely Maureen when I regularly trotted out the hoary chestnut:

'I'm thinking about digging the garden. I'm turning it over in my mind.'

She did not appreciate the feeble attempt at humour, and there were occasions when she almost shamed me into gardening. She would strip off her pinny, pull on her gloves and tear into a back-breaking session of pulling out weeds and stones. There were times when I couldn't bear to watch her enthusiastic onslaught on dandelions, deadly nightshade and all the other creeping pests associated with the stamina-sapping grind of horticultural activities. I often had to walk away from my vantage point behind the front window or even draw the curtains to blot out the sight of the lass struggling with diminishing enthusiasm in her attempts to bring our spacious spread up to a reasonably tidy standard.

I once loaned my garden to Alf, a chap who was potty about growing plants. He too was a genius. His fingers were so green, even the dead sticks he employed to mark off rows of seedlings sprouted buds. Alf left me a cryptic message after one of my rare excursions into our vegetable patch.

I managed to hoe up a line of Alf's spring onions in the belief that they were weeds, and he was not best pleased. In fact he was quite indignant and his feelings were expressed with the instruction: 'Don't meddle with the garden'.

I haven't meddled from that day to this, but I do have a tip for those who are planning to plant a few rows of potatoes to help the family budget. My late father was a dab hand with a dibber. He lived for his garden. The flower beds produced a splash of vivid hues. His back garden yielded the best spuds, cabbages, cauliflowers, carrots ... I almost drool when I think of them. His potatoes were outstanding, and he always planted them on Good Friday. He was not deeply religious. He was not superstitious. But he honestly believed that his potatoes — hanging like bunches of grapes from the roots — owed their massive growth and appetising excellence to the day on which they were sowed.

You don't have to be a genius like Edward Jones, or Alf or me to get the right results.

Christmas in the Desert ... and Tears in my Eyes

'The desert wind blows sand in your eyes
And you can't see the jam on your pudding for flies...'
No self-respecting poet would claim credit for such doggerel,
but it just about sums up the only Christmas I spent in the
arid Middle East. The year was 1951. The location was Abu
Suier, Egypt. And I don't mind admitting that my tears
streamed unashamedly before that festive period drew to a
close.

Soldiers, sailors and airmen in foreign parts will experience
the feeling when Christmas Day dawns. They will suffer extra
pangs of homesickness. They will yearn for that special
family atmosphere, and hanker for the warmth and nearness
of loved ones. And they will wallow in nostalgia and curse the
obscene circumstances which demands their presence in
faraway climes.

I didn't cry when I walked from duty in the RAF station's
signals section on Christmas Eve 1951, and gazed at a navy-
blue sky dotted with a myriad of stars. I didn't weep when I
knelt — with comrades of all denominations — in the tiny
church for the midnight service. We were in Christmas mood.
And our hearts and lungs almost burst with unrestrained joy
as we joined in time-honoured carols thumped out on a tiny
organ with yellowing ivory keys. I didn't shed tears at the
religious ceremony. And I was in great heart when we

returned from our duties to a billet festooned with trimmings and balloons.

We also had a barrack-room bar packed with sufficient Lunatic's Broth to send a squadron of airmen into dreamland for several weeks. We puffed on our free cigarettes, courtesy of Lord Nuffield. We pulled on thick, black cheroots and we popped the caps from Stella Biera, a locally produced chemical beer. It carried a printed warning about excessive use, and it was an instruction the majority of lads — weaned on Tetley or Melbourne ales — invariably ignored. But it was a dangerous beverage.

One of the hit records at this time was *So Tired* sung by an American, Russ Morgan, and one of our lackeys — Mohammed to his neighbours and Vincent to those of us who learned of his secret conversion to Christianity — woke me on Christmas morning with a gentle shaking of the shoulder. Vincent nicknamed me 'Mr Russ', and I remember him murmuring 'Mr Russ, Happy Christmas. It is time to get up.' And a bog-eyed Airman Second Class Morgan J (Number 2392100) prepared for the festive celebrations.

Presents with 'Don't open until Christmas Day' labels had arrived weeks before. They were stowed away in kit bags which were pushed under our respective beds. There was a mad scramble to rip off the coloured paper wrappings, and I probably had a lump in my throat — but no tears — when I read the messages on the cards and murmured silent thanks for the shower of shaving soap, razor blades, brushes, comb, hair cream, socks and underpants which fell from the discarded coverings.

But I admit that I swallowed deeply and my eyes were stinging when I opened a tin from my dear old mum which was packed with a Christmas cake, cheese, boiled ham sandwiches and mince pies. She must have thought that we were starving, so she had carefully sealed the home-made rations in the tin and sent it to Egypt — by boat. It took nine weeks to arrive, and it had probably been stored in the heat just above the engine room. That, and the fact that air had somehow pierced the tin, resulted in the most obnoxious sight and smell imaginable. Even the desert rats — the animal variety — would have fled from the parcel, which was quickly buried, tin and all, in a plot of sand a couple of hundred yards from civilisation.

Of course I immediately wrote thank-you letters, with a special one to my mother to tell her that her most thoughtful present had been a pleasant surprise, welcomed and shared by me with grateful friends. I told her that Christmas would not have been the same without her 'spice cake' and how we had relished the same.

Our RAF officers carved the turkey and served lunch in a temperature well into the 90s, and it seemed incongruous to be tucking into typically English fare under the burning midday sun. We listened to records, with Steve Conway — the Covent Garden porter turned vocalist — crooning *For All You Mean To Me*. We joined Vera Lynn in her tearjerker *The Longest Mile is the Last Mile Home* and, of course, we were dewy-eyed when Bing Crosby's *Silent Night* was played to an equally silent audience.

I didn't cry, though — not even when we bade goodbye to lads who received an unexpected bonus with their presents. One of the officers handed round 'posting notices', and the lucky recipients dashed to pack their gear in preparation for a Christmas departure to Port Said where they caught the good ship *The Devonshire* on its way from the Far East to Liverpool's Mersey Docks. Of course we were envious, but we wished them *bon voyage* and streamed from our humble billet to see them climb on lorries for their journey to the point of embarkation.

Suddenly there was even greater excitement. A railway track ran at the side of our hut. The rails were usually covered with drifted sand because trains were few and far between. We hadn't seen one for months, but in the distance we spotted smoke rising from a chimney and we could hear the steady chug-chug of a steam locomotive. It was a dot in the distance but it came nearer, clearing white powdery sand from rails which gleamed in the glare of the torrid sunshine. On the side of the green and black engine was a brass plate. It was burnished. It had been regularly and lovingly polished. The words almost leaped from the plaque. They read:

'Made at Hunslet Engineering Company, Leeds, Yorkshire.'

It was then I wept. And I cried the proverbial bucketful.